Other Books by David Clarke

Winning the Parenting War

A Marriage After God's Own Heart

I Don't Love You Anymore

MEN ARE CLAMS,

WOMEN ARE CROWBARS

Understand Your Differences
and Make Them Work

DAVID CLARKE, PH.D.

PROMISE PRESS

An Imprint of Barbour Publishing

MEN ARE CLAMS, WOMEN ARE CROWBARS

© 1998 by David Clarke, Ph.D.

ISBN 1-58660-726-X

Published by Promise Press, an imprint of Barbour Publishing, Inc., P.O. Box 719, Uhrichsville, Ohio 44683, www.barbourbooks.com

 Member of the
Evangelical Christian
Publishers Association

Printed in the United States of America.
5 4 3 2 1

ACKNOWLEDGMENTS

Sandy Clarke, the love of my life and the woman who has taught me all I know about marriage.

Emily, Leeann, Nancy, and William Clarke, the four greatest kids in the world. Thanks for giving Dad the time to write.

Bill Clarke, my model, my mentor, and my personal editor.

Kathy Clarke, my biggest fan.

Rocky Glisson, Todd Bates, and Denise Hall—three great friends. Thanks for your prayers and support.

Chuck Milner, you believed in me and gave great advice.

Ethel Harris, a terrific secretary, a godly woman, and a great source of guidance. Thanks also for typing half of the manuscript.

Kathy Schwartz, a wonderful typist and a real encourager.

Joyce Hart, my agent, who guided me through the process.

Susan Schlabach, thanks for liking my work and giving me a chance.

Thom and Lola Provenzola and Larry and Pam Schweizer, I appreciate your friendship and your faith in me.

CONTENTS

INTRODUCTION

Women. Will men ever really understand women? Did you ever notice that most women have a lot of clothes? Dresses, skirts, pants, blouses. And don't forget the accessories: shoes, belts, scarves, things for their hair. The list is endless! Most women have more clothes right now than they could ever possibly wear in one lifetime. But they keep buying more! Why? We don't know.

Take a look at the closet shared by the average couple. Three-quarters of that baby is jammed full of the woman's clothes. If the light is just right and you look real close, you can just barely make out the tiny, cramped section the man is forced to use.

It's not fair! It's not right! And it needs to stop. Ladies, we've had enough. The party's over. I'm starting a new national organization for men. I call it: Take Back The Closet.

Speaking of clothes, there is a situation which has puzzled men for centuries. Here is a woman who owns enough clothes and accessories to outfit a small European country. She stands in front of her closet—and I mean her closet—and in all sincerity says these classic words: "I just don't have a thing to wear." What? You've got to be kidding! The correct statement, my dear, is: "I can't decide what to wear out of the thousands of choices I have."

Another quality about women that men don't understand is the way they talk. Women love details and can remember with astonishing clarity every event of their day. In fact, every event of the past twenty-five years.

This is fine in and of itself. The problem is that a woman wants to share all the details with her man. The man wants the big picture, the overall sketch. He gets drowned in too many details while the woman spends twenty minutes describing what happened, how she felt about it, and how it affected her life. And that's just to cover the time from her car door to the mall entrance. She's just getting started!

For me, as a man, listening to this kind of story is like ordering a pepperoni pizza and having it delivered one pepperoni at a time. Please give me the whole pizza, give it to me now! Get to the point before I die of old age.

We men have also never really understood why women cry and cry so much. Women cry when they're happy. They cry when they're sad. They cry when they're angry. They cry when they're tired. Sometimes they cry and don't even know why. Now, that's spooky.

There is no more pitiful sight in the world than a man whose woman is crying. He doesn't know what to do. Everything he tries seems to backfire and lead to more crying, which is the last thing he wants. If he moves in close and tries to comfort her, she says: "Back off, bud. How dare you touch me! You caused this problem." If he backs off and gives the woman he loves some space, she says: "That's right, ignore me. You never cared."

Well, enough about women. I've been married since 1982 to Sandy, and I have a lot of material, but it's time to get to the men.

Men. Will women ever really understand men? During courtship, the man is the absolute spirit of romance. He's a cross between Ricardo Montalban and Cary Grant: suave, charming, attentive, and caring. His only goal in life is to please his woman. Her every wish is his command. But what happens to a man after marriage? A terrible transformation takes place that his wife can't understand.

After the wedding and a few years into the marriage, things are just a little bit different. The man becomes the absolute spirit of selfishness. He's about as romantic as a wet blanket. His idea of a romantic evening is eating a big, thick steak (that the woman cooks), renting a war movie, and falling asleep on the couch with his hand in the potato chip bag. The poor woman goes from the days of wine and roses to the days of cheeseburgers and dirty underwear. It's a long drop!

Another nasty surprise for women is learning that men don't like to do routine household chores. Laundry, doing the dishes, and vacuuming are beneath men's dignity and position. Men prefer big, glamorous projects like the Panama Canal, buying a new car, remodeling the den, or putting in a sprinkler system. These are jobs that will be noticed and stand the test of time.

Ladies, isn't it amazing how a man who holds a responsible job requiring hard work and a variety of skills can be so lazy and useless at home? When a man comes through the front door, his IQ drops forty points, and he is suddenly unable to operate appliances and perform simple house-cleaning tasks. And when the man does complete a small household chore, what does he immediately expect? You know, ladies. A parade in his honor and the Nobel Peace Prize! If the woman doesn't sink to her knees and thankfully kiss his ring, he pouts. He did a job and no one noticed. Poor thing!

The real capper for women is their frustrated attempts to engage men in deep, personal conversations. Men aren't very good at deep, personal conversations. It seems to women that all men think about is food, their jobs, sports, and sex—not necessarily in that order. Men don't talk much, and when they do open their mouths it's to belch or ask you to pass the mustard.

A woman watches a man express a broad range of intense emotions during a ball game on television: rage, joy, fear, passion. I mean, he's all over the map emotionally. After the game, she asks him how his day was, and he says: "Okay." And the crazy thing is, he expects that one word to satisfy her curiosity. "Oh! It was okay! Thanks for sharing. That tells me so much!"

After years of clinical experience and careful research, I have discovered that most men have a very limited vocabulary after marriage. In fact, the vast majority of married men only utter four statements. "I don't know." "Did you say something, dear?" "I need a shirt for tomorrow." And, of course, the most important statement: "What's for dinner?"

My point with these observations of men and women is that it's very difficult to figure out the opposite sex. Men and women operate on completely different levels most of the time. The way we view relationships, the way we think, and the way we express emotions are all dramatically different. There isn't one major area where the two sexes naturally fit together. Not one!

Why did God do this to us? Why did He make us so different? Besides having a sense of humor, I believe there are three main reasons.

First, our differences force us to depend on God. Without God, marriage is impossible. God wants to be at the center of man-woman relationships, so He created a relationship so difficult that we have to keep Him there to make it work.

Second, our differences can lead to a complementary relationship. The man and the woman each contribute unique qualities that, together, can make a balanced whole.

Third, our differences can lead to deep intimacy. Because we are so different, we can come together again and again in a limitless number of physical, emotional, and spiritual combinations. Same-sex friendships are important and can be very close but will never be as deep as a heterosexual marriage. The deepest and best human intimacy comes between a man and a woman.

You'll notice that I said these differences can lead to these benefits. They can also tear a relationship apart. Many opposite-sex relationships fail because the partners do not learn how to deal effectively with their basic male-female differences.

We start every interaction—and I mean every interaction—on two different levels. If we are to get beneath the surface and really connect as a couple, we must understand our differences. We must see how our differences affect our conversations. And we must learn specific techniques that will enable us to work with our differences to create a deep, lasting intimacy.

ONE

GOOD LUCK, BETTY!

Use your imagination and picture this scenario. I'll bet you'll recognize it. We have two persons in a relationship: Bob and Betty. Near the end of one day, Betty is attempting to develop a conversation with Bob. You see, Betty wants to learn more about Bob, to get him to share some personal information. And so, she asks him some questions.

"How was your day?"

"What are you thinking about right now?"

"How do you feel?"

(Women love to ask these questions, and it drives men

crazy.) Betty is probing, trying to get inside the man she loves. She wants to know Bob better. She wants to reach him on a deeper level. Good luck, Betty!

To Betty's dismay and growing irritation, Bob does not provide any personal information. He becomes very defensive and acts as though he's being tortured by the secret police. He's holding Betty at arm's length and won't talk personally. In response to Betty's questions, Bob grunts a few times (we men are good at this), makes some vague statements, and falls silent. He's not going to talk!

Betty isn't satisfied with this reaction at all. She wants more than grunts in her marriage! She wants talking, dialogue, sharing, and closeness. Betty presses for some response, and Bob finally gets angry, snaps at her verbally, and leaves the room. Both end up angry, hurt, and confused.

A CLASSIC
MALE-FEMALE INTERACTION

This scenario is not new for Bob and Betty. It has happened many times before and, unless they learn what's causing it, it will continue to happen. And each time it happens, they've lost another opportunity for intimacy.

This is a classic male-female interaction, isn't it? The woman asks questions and tries desperately to get the man to open up. She's the crowbar. The man resists her attempts and does not open up. He shuts down. He pulls in. He's the clam.

I'm convinced this crowbar-clam interaction has been happening between men and women ever since Adam and Eve sinned and left the Garden of Eden. I can picture the

scene as they leave the garden. Eve wants to talk abo
happened. She wants to express herself and find o
Adam feels about the whole thing. Adam doesn't
talk about it. "Eve, give me a break, will you? It's been a bad
day, we can't change what happened, and I have nothing else
to say. Let's just find a place to camp tonight."

Keep in mind that in this crowbar-clam scenario, there
is no good guy and bad guy. Neither person is acting maliciously with the intent to hurt the other. What's happening
is two persons operating on completely different levels
without realizing it.

WHY ARE WE SO DIFFERENT?

Why are women crowbars? Why do they pry and prod and
probe for personal information from their men? All the men
are thinking: *Yeah, why do they do that?* I'll tell you why.

In a relationship women want closeness. That's their
number one priority. For a woman, if she has no closeness
in a relationship she has nothing. She literally can't be happy
and satisfied.

Why are men clams? Why do they shut down and deny
the women they love what they want and need? All the
women are thinking: *Tell me, please. I've always wondered
why.* I'll tell you why.

In a relationship, men want control. That's their number
one priority. For a man, if he has no control in a relationship
he has nothing.

Men and women operate on these different levels, control and closeness, because of two main reasons. One, it's
simply genetic. We're born to operate these two ways. Two—

and this is the real clincher—we're taught to throughout our upbringing.

We men are taught from birth to develop these qualities in our relationships: respect, status, strength, power, and independence. These are all qualities designed to produce control.

Do you ever watch little boys when they play? It's a violent, competitive, dog-eat-dog jungle. Who won, who got the most hits, who killed the most enemies with his Rambo gun, who scored the winning points? It's a battle to see who is the strongest, the fastest, the best. There is very little talking. Only grunts, car noises, and yelling.

And what little boy hasn't been told "Men don't cry"? That's weakness. Don't express your true feelings and thoughts. That will give your opponent the edge. Gotta be cool under pressure, gotta be calm in a crisis, gotta be in control. This message is drilled into us, and we learn it.

Our cultural heroes are men like John Wayne and Clint Eastwood. In their movies, John and Clint are tough, hard-bitten customers. They waste no words, and they show little or no emotion. Oddly enough, the women in these movies are all over John and Clint. These ladies seem perfectly satisfied with several grunts and a couple of twitches from their men over the course of a day. In the real world, any woman would be unhappy and downright bored with this type of man.

Women are taught from birth to develop these qualities in relationships: connection, cooperation, openness, understanding, and intimacy. Wow, what a difference! These are all qualities designed to produce closeness.

When little girls play, it's a more peaceful and cooperative environment. I ought to know. I have three daughters. They don't try to kill each other or fight to prove who's the best. They work together. They consider how others think and feel. There's a lot of talking, and the talking is all focused on getting to know each other. The play of little girls is relationship-oriented.

Let me illustrate with how my three girls play Barbies with me. They lead me to the clubhouse, a big room in our home where all the toys are kept. I'm faced with a big pile of forty-five naked Barbies. (It's a little overwhelming.) The first thing we each have to do is select one Barbie that each of us will be. When you choose your Barbie, you become that Barbie for the duration of the game. You will talk and act through that Barbie. You and your Barbie become one.

Then, we have to dress our Barbies because they're naked. Ever dressed a Barbie? You'd think it would be a snap, since Barbie is so unbelievably skinny. Guess again. Barbie is extremely thin, but her clothes are even thinner. It takes twenty minutes just to tug on a top and a pair of pants! And when the last Barbie is finally dressed, the rule is, every Barbie has to feel good about every other Barbie's outfit. If even one of the other Barbies doesn't think I look good in my outfit, my Barbie has to change. "Oh, Barbie, those green shorts just don't go with that pink top." My Barbie tries to argue, but inevitably, I put on what my Barbie friends feel looks best on me.

Finally, all the Barbies are dressed and happy. Now comes the real challenge—at least for me. The Barbies have to decide where to go in their nice clothes. Again, all the Barbies have to feel good about the decision, or it doesn't happen. Each Barbie mentions where she would like to go, and then the entire group discusses the idea. If all the Barbies don't agree, they go nowhere.

My Barbie says: "Let's go to the beach." Barbie Number

Two says: "Yes." Barbie Number Three says: "Yes." Barbie Number Four says: "No, I don't want to. I might get sunburned." So, the deal's off! Undaunted, my Barbie tosses her head back, stretches both her bony arms out, and says: "It's three votes to one. We're going to the beach. If you don't want to go, tough! Stay here." Oh, no! That's not how sensitive, relationship-oriented little girls operate. The other Barbies say to my Barbie: "No. We all have to agree, or we can't go. You know that." In all the years I've played Barbies, we've never actually gone anywhere!

Emily, Leeann, and Nancy would rather sit around on the floor of the clubhouse talking about where to go than go somewhere and have even one Barbie not feel good about it. My point? That's women.

And let's not forget, for girls, it's okay to cry. In fact, it's important and expected to open up and tell secrets because this will lead to closeness. And closeness is what little girls want.

Eventually, little boys and little girls grow up, but how they operate in relationships stays exactly the same. So when men and women come together in conversation, there isn't just the potential for trouble. Oh, no! There is an absolute guarantee of trouble!

Some of you are thinking: *Hey, wait a minute. In our relationship, these roles are reversed. The man is the crowbar, and the woman is the clam. Are we strange? Are we deviant?*

Well, you might be strange but not for this reason. Don't worry. Don't panic. You're perfectly normal. In 20 to 25 percent of couples, there is a flip-flop of these roles and the woman has difficulty expressing her personal thoughts and feelings. She often shuts down in conversation; she's the clam. The man is more expressive by nature and wants to develop deeper conversations with the woman. He tries, without success, to get her to talk; he's the crowbar.

You couples in this reversed position will find this book just as helpful as couples in the more common position. The same principles apply. Just reverse the sexes.

TWO

INCOMING! INCOMING!

I love old western movies. I love everything about them. Dusty streets. Cowboys. Outlaws. Cattle drives. Posses. Frontier justice. Gunfights. The Old West was an exciting place filled with adventure, drama, and real men. Gary Cooper and John Wayne may not have known how to treat women, but they sure knew how to get rid of the bad guys.

My wife, Sandy, does not share my enthusiasm for westerns. Sandy, like most women, wants a movie with a lot of romance. She wants witty, deep dialogue between a man and a woman. She wants long, drawn out emotional scenes. I want bodies in the streets.

Every western worth its salt has at least one scene in a

saloon where the good guy and the bad guy meet and have a showdown. Nobody dies in this scene—that comes later in the final gunfight—but it's pretty uncomfortable.

The good guy is at the bar sipping his rye whiskey. (Real men, at least real men in old westerns, drink only rye whiskey.) Suddenly, the bad guy comes swaggering into the bar through those neat, swinging bar doors. The two men make eye contact and, at the same instant, draw their guns. Neither man has the advantage, so neither one shoots. They just stand there, a few feet apart, pointing their six-shooters at each other. You can cut the tension with a knife. It is a classic Mexican standoff. Why they call it a Mexican stand-off, I don't know. The point is, nothing happens. No action can be taken.

Just like these western characters, men and women get into Mexican standoffs all the time. We don't end up using guns. For us, these are conversation standoffs. We adopt, unconsciously and automatically, two diametrically opposed positions in most of our conversations. The result is absolute and complete gridlock. Neither partner budges. There is no connection. There is no communication. There is no intimacy. The two guys in the saloon with the guns trained on each other have a better chance of resolving their standoff than a man and a woman do in getting past a conversation standoff.

Here we have adult Bob, who has a built-in alarm system to warn him of incoming threats to his control, and adult Betty, the guided missile, who's going to get closeness if it's the last thing she does. It's not a good combination. In fact, it's a standoff waiting to happen. Let's take a look at what is happening inside the man and woman during a classic Mexican standoff conversation.

What's Happening Inside Bob?

What is Bob, the clam, really thinking and feeling as his partner asks him to talk?

When Betty asks Bob to open up and share what's inside, his alarm goes off, and he automatically responds with defensive maneuvers. He doesn't even know why he's doing it! His responses are unconscious reflexes. It's what he's always done in this situation.

Deep down, Bob believes that sharing secrets will make him vulnerable and weak. With a man, in the business world, it would! But not with his woman. Not with his precious, lifelong lover! But he doesn't know that because Bob has never—literally never—seen a man he was close to open up and share deeply with a woman. He never saw his dad do it. He never saw Grandpa do it. He never saw Uncle Harry do it.

If Dad ever did share himself personally with Mom, it was behind closed doors. Bob did see his dad stiffen up and resist Mom's attempts at conversation a million times. So, in addition to his cultural training, Bob learned from his dad that you keep your guard up with a woman. Bob thinks if he opens up to Betty, he risks getting hurt and getting dominated. Most of all, he thinks he risks losing control.

Let's see this in action: After a bad day at work, a man will get home and make a beeline for his wife. He'll say: "Honey, I had a bad day and need to pour my heart out to you!" Is this what happens? Are you kidding? Never! He won't appear out of control, or weak, or vulnerable.

When a woman asks a man how his day was, he'll give her one of several stock replies. He'll say: "Fine." Fine? What does fine mean? Or, he'll say: "Okay." Wow, that tells her a lot. Or, he'll answer: "Not bad." Well, that narrows it down. At least she can rule out bad.

All these answers are safe responses which tell the woman nothing and keep the man in control. Every man is a master at sidestepping questions and holding back the information and feelings the woman wants.

The woman can sense something is not quite right in the man. He's tense, quieter than usual. Her intuition is usually right on, for all the good it'll do her. Her chances of extracting the truth, what's inside, are practically nil. She has a better chance of winning the lottery or being the first woman on Mars. Nevertheless, she'll ask him a question when she already knows the answer: "Is there anything bothering you?" And he replies: "No." Big fat lie number one. She tries again, being a little more direct: "What's wrong, honey?" He answers: "Nothing." Big fat lie number two.

If the man provides any information at all, it is precious little and usually just intended to get the woman off his back. At the most, he'll say: "Well, I had a bad day, that's all. But. . .I don't want to talk about it." Big fat cop-out.

Getting back to Bob: He may also fear that he won't do well if he shares personally. The woman is much better at this personal sharing stuff, and if he can't win or do well, he won't try. It's an old lesson we men are taught as we grow up: Never, ever, let a woman beat you at anything. It's a stupid lesson, but it's taught, and we learn it.

If Bob's elementary school was anything like mine, the worst thing that could happen to a boy was being beaten at any sport or physical contest by a girl! If a girl beat you in a race, or did more chin-ups on the six-foot bar, your name was mud. It was the ultimate humiliation. You'd hear the teasing and snide comments from the other guys for weeks. Now, I don't remember getting beaten by a girl, but I can still picture those poor guys who failed this ridiculous caveman test of elementary-age manhood.

Because of Bob's incorrect beliefs and intense drive to remain in control, he does one of three things in response to Betty's attempts to open him up.

1. Bob may become silent. (Like the Sergeant Schultz character in the old *Hogan's Heroes* television show, he knows nothing, and he sees nothing—and, in Bob's case, he says nothing.)

2. Bob may get angry and snap verbally at Betty.

3. He may physically leave the situation.

Of course, Bob may do all three. Whatever his response, the conversation is over.

WHAT'S HAPPENING INSIDE BETTY?

What is Betty, the crowbar, thinking and feeling as she tries unsuccessfully to pry the clam open?

Betty watches Bob go into the clam routine and works her crowbar harder and faster. She escalates; she gets more intense because she sees the closeness she wants slipping away. Betty thinks and may actually verbalize: "Talk to me! I want to help. I want to know you. I want to be your soul mate. I want to connect with you. Stop being the Lone Ranger." She may say, as one client of mine did to her husband: "If I wanted company without conversation, I'd live with a dog, a cat, an iguana!"

When a woman has a bad day, she can't wait to talk about it—with her husband, her mother, some close friends, even the woman she just met in the grocery store line. She always feels better after expressing herself. Naturally, if her man has had a bad day, the woman cannot understand his refusal to talk about it. She'll say to him: "Honey, it'll help to talk about it. You'll get it off your chest, and you won't be as stressed." It blows her mind that he chooses, again and again, to hold in stress and hurt himself. Does he enjoy pain?

The woman is also naturally curious and is dying to know what happened to the man today. She lives in a world of details and can't ever get enough. Women want to know everything that's going on in the lives of their loved ones. Even the smallest event, the most trivial tidbit, is of interest and collected. The woman then uses all these details in her nurturing role.

If she learns what's happened to her husband, she believes she can help him. And. . .she's right! Maybe she can say something to help. Maybe she can do something to help. Maybe she can touch him, support him, encourage him. Maybe she can be his soul mate. But when her man won't talk about his troubles, all these maybes end up as a little pile of conversational sawdust on the floor.

She becomes a nurturer without a "nurturee." There's nothing quite as frustrating for a nurturer than to be denied the opportunity to nurture. She knows he's upset. She can feel his pain. She wants desperately to find out what has gone wrong with him so she can nurture him. If he won't tell her, there's nothing she can do. That's incredibly frustrating. It also hurts her. She feels rejected because she thinks her own husband doesn't trust her enough to open up to her.

When in conversation, a woman—a Betty—hits a brick

wall with her man, she doesn't give up easily. When he won't talk about his bad day or just plain won't talk personally, Betty thinks inside: *If I just push hard enough, I'll break through.*

Wrong. Dead wrong. He'll clam up even tighter.

I have carefully checked all known historical records, using libraries, encyclopedias, the Internet, and a lot of really old people. There is no recorded incident of a man breaking down under a woman's questioning and sharing any personal information.

Sorry Betty, your husband will not be the first.

Betty also thinks: *Bob knows I want closeness, and he is deliberately denying it to me.* It's a small jump to her next few thoughts: *He doesn't care about me. He doesn't even really love me.*

All you Bettys: Listen to me. You are wrong. I understand this thinking, but it's still wrong. Unless you married a sociopath, your husband is not deliberately and maliciously holding back closeness from you. He does care about you. He doesn't know how to love you the way you need to be loved yet, but he does love you.

What's happening when he clams up and will not let you inside is that his control is threatened, and he can't let that happen. Just as you don't mean to threaten his control, he doesn't mean to hurt you with his clam response.

THREE

CLAMS AND CROWBARS ALL OVER THE PLACE

A man in his early fifties goes to see his family doctor for his annual physical. He tells the doctor he feels fine, never better, and expects to get his usual clean bill of health. This time, that doesn't happen. This time his rectal exam, that unpleasant procedure men over forty must endure, reveals an enlarged prostate. "Not to worry," the doctor says. "It's probably nothing serious, but I'm ordering some tests." The tests bring bad news: cancer of the prostate. Further tests bring more bad news: It has spread and invaded several major organs. Surgery and chemotherapy do not work, and the man dies six months after his physical.

He felt fine! He had no idea that cancer was growing inside him. If he'd only known what was happening, he would have seen the doctor earlier, and immediate treatment might have saved him.

Just like this unfortunate man, every married couple has an unseen enemy eating away at their relationship. I hate to sound so morbid, but it's true. The signs are all there. You both know your intimacy could be better. Your conversations could be deeper. Your passion—well, it isn't what it used to be. But you can't put your finger on the reason. You don't know why. And you can't fight something if you don't know what it is.

I'll tell you why your relationship isn't what it could be. You are being attacked by the relationship disease known as control and closeness. And it is slowly killing your love. The reason this disease is so devastating is because couples don't even realize it's there. They don't see how it works day after day, week after week, year after year, in so many different ways.

The bad news is you and your mate are doing the control and closeness thing every day, and it's killing your relationship. The good news is you bought this book, and you're about to find out how to identify and defeat this disease.

To successfully conquer an enemy, you must first find out what it is, and how it operates. When you start looking for it, you'll notice this control and closeness problem operating in many of your interactions.

PLEASE DO YOUR CHORES

See if you recognize this scene. The woman asks the man to do a chore around the house. The man smiles and says: "Honey, I'd be happy to help you. It's the least I can do in return for all you've done for me." And he jumps right up and does that chore.

Is that the way it happens in your home? I don't think so. The man resists and fights against doing the chore! He won't do it right away when you ask. He'd be your servant! He'd be nothing more than a puppet on a string! He'd be a mama's boy!

Some men will flatly refuse to do the chore, but that's pretty rare. Most men will say: "Sure, honey, I'll do it later." What happens to "later," ladies? Later never comes. The man forgets or waits so long to do it that the woman feels forced to remind him. When she reminds him, he sees her as a nag, and he resists doing the chore all the more. He fails to realize that she wouldn't have to nag if he'd get the chore done in a reasonable time frame.

Often, the woman will get tired of waiting and do the chore herself. She doesn't want to nag, and the job needs to get done. And as soon as the man sees her doing the chore, he says: "Oh, come on, honey! I was just about to do that!" Yeah, right.

What's going on here? Why does the man react so defensively to a simple request by the woman to do a chore? Why does it turn into a tense, negative situation? I'll tell you what's going on. It's the same old clam-crowbar, control-closeness problem.

The woman sees the chore as a way to achieve closeness. Now, she needs the help anyway. Taking care of a home or apartment is too big a job for one person. Household chores aren't just the woman's job. Chores ought to be shared equally by the two partners in a marriage. But what the woman is really after is closeness. When her man helps with the household chores, she feels closer to him. She feels as though they are a team. She feels as though they are working together. She feels as though he really cares about her!

Ladies, am I right? Yes, of course I'm right.

The home is very important to a woman. No matter how small or humble, the home is her nest. It is her pride and joy. She is emotionally connected to every single item in her home. She knows where everything is, and she knows all the jobs that need to be done.

Men, when you are taking care of your home, you are taking care of your woman. If her man doesn't help with the chores, she feels distant from him. He just sleeps here. He's just a consumer living off the fat of the land. She feels alone, terribly alone, in her own home.

What's the matter with this slug of a man? Why is he resisting this good-hearted woman whom he loves? Is he lazy? Is he cruel? Is he mean? No. He's resisting the chore because his control and independence are being challenged. Or, at least he thinks they are. Deep down, the man's automatic response is: "I won't be told what to do."

It may sound crazy, but the man will risk hurting his woman, causing her emotional pain and physical fatigue, to protect his control. If his boss orders him to do a job, no matter how nasty it is, he'll do it. His control isn't threatened because he understands the chain of command. If his dear wife asks him to do a job, he interprets it as an order and he digs in his heels.

COME AND GET IT!

Here's another control-closeness scenario that happens in every home on a regular basis.

The woman has made the meal and calls the man to the table: "Come and get it! Time to eat, honey!" What does the man do? He stalls. He takes his time. He'll come when he's ready. He unconsciously refuses to come immediately and piddles around for a few minutes.

Suddenly, whatever activity the man is doing when he's called becomes extremely important. It becomes an issue of national security. He simply must take a few minutes to finish up or people will die. If he's watching television, the commercial he's watching becomes incredibly interesting. It's the laundry detergent commercial he's seen a million times. But he has to watch the end. Maybe this time the clothes won't get clean!

If he's puttering around in the garage, he'll keep puttering for just a little while. Just long enough to prove he is an independent man who can't be controlled. "When I hang up my hammer on that peg, then I'll go to the table. On my terms. Just like John Wayne. Just like Clint Eastwood. Nobody calls me. I come when I want."

The woman wants closeness when she calls him to the table. Mealtime isn't just about food. It's a time for family, for connecting, and for togetherness. It's time for closeness. She wants the man to come right away so they can get to the closeness she needs. "Come in, honey, and let's share our lives." For the man—he has heard an order and instantly feels controlled. Silly? Yes. Crazy? Maybe. But it's reality. It's how men operate.

What can we do about this control-closeness problem?

What can we do to keep it from killing our daily interactions and conversations? Let's look at some practical ideas that defeat this problem, cure this disease, and lead to deeper communication. These strategies have not only helped my wife, Sandy, and me, but many couples I've worked with in therapy and in my seminars.

FOUR

EXCUSE ME, BUT YOU'RE DOING IT AGAIN!

I have an annoying habit. Actually, I have more than one, but space doesn't permit me to describe all of them. This habit is one I've had for years, and it is so ingrained I don't even know when I'm doing it. It's automatic. It's totally unconscious. Unfortunately, it drives my dear wife crazy. Right up the wall.

I hum, over and over and over, the last song I hear. It might be on the radio, a commercial jingle on the television, or a song playing on our CD player at home. It must be some kind of genetic curse. That last piece of music sticks in my head, and I start humming it all day long. Of course, I never know the whole song. That's the really annoying part. I hum the few bars and sing the handful of words I remember. . .over and over. I may hate the song. I may have heard the song only once. It makes no difference. I'm going to hum and sing my tiny remembered fragment until I hear another song. Then, I start over with that one.

Sandy is a patient woman, but even she has her limits. She doesn't mind if I hum and sing around other people, but she really doesn't want to hear my little repeated performances. So, she began an antihumming campaign. She made it clear that either I stopped the habit, or she'd have to kill me. I thought she was joking, but the look on her face made me wonder.

Since there isn't a Betty Ford Center for Annoying Hummers, Sandy and I tackled the problem ourselves. Sandy's first idea was simply to ask me to stop. Maybe if I was made aware of my problem, that would be enough to help me stop. However, just knowing I was annoying her, and deciding to stop, weren't enough. The humming continued, so the second idea was for me to catch myself humming and stop. Great idea, except for one small problem. I didn't even know I was doing it. How can you catch yourself humming when you don't know you're humming?

Our final idea has been the solution. Sandy, who always knows when I begin humming, verbally points it out to me. Sometimes she's even nice about it. When she interrupts me, I realize what I'm doing and can stop. Now, I may only stop for an hour or two, but at least she gets a break. When I start humming again, she interrupts me again with the phrase: "Dave, you're humming." Our marriage has been saved, and my life spared.

Verbal Interruption

To battle the control-closeness problem, the technique of verbal interruption is the first idea I suggest. It won't be enough on its own, but it's a key part of the solution. Both partners agree to verbally bring up the control-closeness problem when it occurs in conversation. In other words, catch yourselves in the act!

A very effective way to break an entrenched pattern is to point it out right when it is happening. Or, as soon as possible. Ideally, you both agree this pattern is hurting your relationship, and you team up against it. This way you bring the automatic—the unconscious—behavior to the conscious. You bring it out into the open. If the pattern stays hidden, you're dead. It will always win, and you will always lose. If you don't point out the control-closeness problem, you are doomed to play out the same old clam-crowbar scenario.

What's Happening in You?

There are a couple of ways to point out the problem. First, you can mention what's happening inside of you. This is learning to catch yourself. During a conversation, you notice what's going on in you, and you mention it to your partner. When you feel controlled by your wife, you say so. You could say: "Honey, I feel controlled right now, and I'm getting defensive and angry." This isn't a whole lot of fun for the woman to hear, but it stops the pattern cold.

If the clam says nothing, that is, he does not catch himself, he will have no choice but to use one of his old, reliable tools to get out of the conversation. He'll shut down and be silent. Or he'll snap at her. Or he'll leave the situation phys-ically. But if he tells his wife that he feels controlled, a lot of good things can happen. The pattern is interrupted. His anger, which was building, is released and drains away. Best of all, a conversation that was going nowhere (except to a brick wall) can be restarted and put back on track.

The woman also can bring up what's going on inside of her. She could say: "Bob, I really want closeness now, and I'm pushing too hard for it, aren't I?" Bob will say: "Yes, ma'am. You're all over me." If the crowbar can catch herself working the man over, the conversation can be salvaged. The alternative is feeling increasing levels of frustration and hurt as the clam holds his shell together.

WHAT'S HAPPENING IN YOUR PARTNER?

The second way to point out the control-closeness problem is to mention what you see happening in your partner. Feedback like this is important because you can seldom catch yourself doing something, especially a weakness. (Like humming, for example. You know how it is.) You can, how-ever, almost always see a weakness in your partner.

Catching your partner erecting a conversational road-block will work, as long as you are very careful in your approach. Tread softly, and be gentle. No sarcasm or critical tone or arrogant attitude is allowed. Unless you want to make a bad situation far worse, you work toward "speaking the truth in love," just as Paul teaches in Ephesians 4:15 (NAS). Your attitude is not: "Gotcha! You're doing something wrong." Rather, your attitude is just the opposite: "Honey, you're doing something that isn't helping our conversation. Let's start over."

Let me illustrate. When the woman sees the man start to clam up, she could say: "Bob, I feel as though you're going into your control mode now. I want some closeness, and you're pulling away." This is better than her saying: "I'm sick of you not talking. Talk to me! Talk to me now!"

It's a good idea to ask your man to give you a statement you can use when he's being a clam. If it's his statement, the one he gave you to use, chances are better he'll respond to it without being hostile and defensive. Agree on this statement before you are in a situation when you have to use it. Also, letting him tell you what statement to use allows him to remain in control. He has decided how you will interrupt him. And remember, with a man, control is critical.

When the man sees the crowbar in action, and she's not catching herself, he needs to say something to stop her. Again, it's a good idea for the man to ask the woman for a statement he can use with her. Fair is fair. He could say something like this: "Betty, you are pressing too hard for closeness now. Your intensity is backing me off." This statement can stop Betty in her tracks and prevent Bob, her clam, from withdrawing into his shell.

As you begin doing this verbal interruption, it will be awkward and difficult. In fact, many times the control-closeness scenario will automatically run its course. It will happen so fast, it'll be over before you can interrupt it. One or both of you will recognize what happened afterwards. That's all right. That's perfectly normal.

AFTER A CONVERSATION

When you realize you fell into the control-closeness trap again, it's not too late to bring it up. Better late than never. You can learn another lesson from an old control-closeness conversation, whether it happened twenty minutes ago or two hours ago.

Talk about what happened. "Honey, did you notice what we did this morning? It was the same old clam-crowbar thing that the brilliant Dr. Clarke describes in his book. Let's talk about it."

Then you go back and briefly recreate the conversation. You examine how each of you responded to the other. You admit the mistakes you made, and you apologize for them. You talk about how you could have communicated differently.

Finally—and this is important—you try the same conversation again and see if you can do better. It's like getting back on a horse after you've fallen off. You take a few minutes to think about what went wrong, then you jump back on. This is how you bury the old pattern and build the new, healthy one. You learn nothing if you just attempt to move on and never revisit the old conversation. So, go back and discuss what you both did wrong. Start again, from the top, watching for the control-closeness routine. You need the practice. It will pay off. With enough repetition, you'll learn how to avoid the same old trouble and actually complete a decent practice conversation.

As you improve, you'll both get better at noticing what goes wrong. The time from the end of the conversation to when one of you realizes what happened will be shorter and shorter. Pretty soon, you'll be able to point out the problem during an actual conversation.

DURING A CONVERSATION

It's easier to look back at an old conversation than to handle the intensity of a current one. When you interrupt your partner in the middle of a conversation, it's more difficult to negotiate the process of examining mistakes and restarting the conversation. But if you both follow some basic guidelines, breaking into a conversation is a powerful way to improve communication.

First, just as in dealing with an old conversation, the partner who brings up the problem must be careful. Be gentle, but firm. Use the corrective statement your partner has given you to use. Your goal is not to humiliate, but to heal.

Second, the partner who is interrupted must show grace under fire. You need to believe that what your partner is telling you is the truth. When you're caught being a clam or a crowbar, be big enough to admit it. It's not pleasant to hear; as a matter of fact, it'll make you mad. Choke back your defensive or offensive reply, swallow your pride, and agree with your partner. Unless you're married to a pathological liar or master manipulator, you are doing what your partner says you are doing.

Don't fight about it: "You're being a clam." "I am not." "Are too." "Am not." When you're called on your pattern, accept it with as much grace as you can muster. "Well, I don't like it. But if you say I'm acting like a clam, I guess I am."

The third guideline is take a short break just after the problem is pointed out. Feelings are running high, especially in the partner who has been called on the conversational carpet. Agree to take a five- to ten-minute break and then come back to continue the conversation. Go to the bathroom, get a drink, or go outside for some fresh air. This cooling off period signals the end of the previous, unhealthy conversation and the beginning of a new, healthy conversation. The intensity level, especially in the partner who was interrupted, is lowered, and the two of you are prepared to start over.

The fourth and final step is starting the conversation again. You come back together after the break and talk about what just happened. You do this to kill the old pattern and, more importantly, to reach a different level on which you can genuinely communicate.

For example, the woman could say: "I'm sorry for being the crowbar. You're right, I was giving you the third degree. Honey, I just want to be close to you and love you."

If the man hears this, it helps. It really does. Not only can he forgive her for being a crowbar, but he can understand why she was one. He doesn't have to feel threatened now, because she doesn't want control. She just wants closeness. The conversation begins again with a whole new frame: a woman and a man trying to be close.

The man could say: "Sorry for clamming up. I felt pressured and, as usual, shut down. I do love you, but I find it hard to let you see what's inside. I don't really want to shut you out."

If the woman hears this, it helps. He didn't clam up because he wanted to hurt or reject her. Or because he doesn't love her. He clammed up because he felt pressured, and he had trouble sharing himself. The conversation begins again with the partners on a new, deeper level. Their new approach is to find a way for the man to share himself freely, without feeling forced to do it.

As you practice catching yourselves in the control-closeness mode, two very nice things will happen. First, you'll find that you do this unhealthy pattern less often. Being aware of a problem and regularly interrupting its operation is effective prevention. Why get cancer and hope to recover, when you can prevent it in the first place?

Since we're not in heaven yet and nobody's perfect, you will continue to get caught in this control-closeness gridlock. But—and here's the second nice thing—with practice, you will become skilled at handling it. When it happens, it won't stop you cold and ruin your day like it used to. You'll fix it and have a good chance to move on to that precious condition we all got married to experience: intimacy.

FIVE

MEN, OPEN UP YOUR CLAMS!

Men like challenges.

In sports, we root for the athlete who seems to have no chance for victory. Injuries and exhaustion have taken their toll, and he can't win, the commentators sadly report. Or can he? Through sheer grit and determination, he does not give up, and he wins the event. *That's a real man,* we think to ourselves.

In business, we admire men who have overcome tremendous odds and seemingly insurmountable hardships to achieve financial success. In our own careers, we'll do whatever it takes to succeed. We'll work long hours, put up with bosses who are unreasonable, and suffer all manner of indignities and defeats. We keep going because we're naturally competitive and want to find out just how good we can be at what we do. We also want to provide the best possible life for our families.

In home improvement projects, we struggle past obstacle after obstacle in our grim determination to get the job done. What could be more frustrating than making twenty trips to the home improvement store, and still not have the right part? We think the "experts" in these glorified hardware superstores who confidently hand you the wrong part ought to be taken out and shot. And then fired. But we press on, because we like to measure ourselves against a real challenge. We will not be defeated.

Our innate drive to succeed in the face of unpredictable and complex obstacles does not, however, apply to our marriages. We tend to wimp out with our wives, don't we? We feel helpless. We feel powerless. We don't seem to have the tools to successfully connect with a woman on a deeper level. It's not that we don't want to. We do want to. We have the same God-given need to be intimate with one member of the opposite sex as women do. But because we are so totally out of our element with a woman, we think there's no way to achieve success, and at the same time maintain control.

So what do we do? When things get a little too personal or a little too difficult with our wives, what's our reaction? Well, like true leaders, we take action and we don't stop trying until we get the job done. Right? Hardly. We quit. We back off. We throw in the towel. We make lame excuses. We give up and shut the woman out. We work harder at our jobs. We throw ourselves into sports. We concentrate on home improvement jobs. These areas are comfortable, and we believe we have a much better chance to succeed in them.

Men, I am as guilty as any man reading these words, so I'm not throwing stones. I know what it's like to believe, to really believe, that I can't communicate and connect with Sandy. What I was ignoring, and what you may still be ignoring, is what God says about love and marriage.

God says love does the difficult things. It's not love to do what is easy, what comes naturally. It's love to do what is hard and unnatural. And, loving a woman the way she needs to be loved is certainly hard and unnatural. She needs her man to be open and vulnerable and to talk on a deeper level. That's just great, you say! That's about the toughest thing for me to do.

God said it all, through the apostle Paul, in Ephesians 5:25: "Husbands, love your wives, just as Christ also loved the church and gave Himself up for her" (NAS). This is the highest possible standard of love.

Jesus Christ sacrificed everything, including His life, for us. He never gave up. He moved past every obstacle in His drive to love us. He is our example. We are to be just like Him as husbands. Are we up to it?

Men, the greatest challenge in life is communicating with a woman on a deeper level. When we meet this challenge and succeed, there's also no greater reward. With God's wisdom, the right information, and hard work, we can get it done.

If you know God through Jesus Christ, you have His help, if you ask. The marvelous promise for us is: "But if any of you lacks wisdom, let him ask of God, who gives to all men generously and without reproach, and it will be given to him" (James 1:5, NAS). His wisdom can be yours.

And you have the right information, because you have this book. Now, we get to the hard work part.

As men, we succeed when we act—when we move forward in decisive ways. No man ever earned success by being defensive and retreating. We are God's ordained leaders in the marriage relationship. (Notice, *leaders,* not bosses!) What that means is we ought to be leading the way in the battle against the control-closeness problem.

So, climb out of your clams, and start acting like leaders. There are two things I want you to do—actually, God wants you to do them; I'm just the messenger. They will be difficult, perhaps two of the most difficult things you have ever done. But when you master these skills, and are doing them regularly, they will make all the difference in your marriage. You will be fulfilling Ephesians 5:25.

Learn to Share Personally with Your Woman

Men, sharing personally with your wife is not an option. It's not an extra. It's an absolute necessity. You can't—literally can't—have a good marriage without it. You can get along. You can be okay. But if you want more to your relationship, you need to open up. It's your job to meet your spouse's needs, and this need is one of her deepest. If you don't share personally, your woman will never feel really loved by you! You don't believe me? Ask her right now. Ask her today. Go on—ask her!

Many men in my therapy office tell me: "Dave, I do love my wife. What difference does it make if I don't share personally with her?" I respond: "It makes all the difference to her."

You only truly love someone when you express that love

in the way that person needs it expressed. Let your woman define how you are to love her. Her definition will be: "Talk to me. Share with me who you really are, what you really think, what you really feel."

You can trust her. She's safe. She's not trying to control you when she wants you to talk or do something for her. All she wants is closeness. Burn this into your frontal lobes: "My wife wants closeness, not control."

Opening up won't make you weak, dominated, and dependent. The first time you share personally, you won't end up on the floor with her foot on your chest. She won't laugh out loud and say: "I'm in charge now." What *will* happen is she will love and respect you. She'll feel closer to you. She'll feel loved by you. And she'll return that love to you in all the nice ways that only a woman can.

She won't tell anyone your secrets, the personal things you share. (Ladies, make sure you keep your mouth shut. If he overhears you reporting to your mother or a friend things he told you, it'll be another five years before he talks to you again.) A good wife is the perfect person to talk to. It's one of the wonderful things she's there to do!

Men, talking to your woman is also good for you. It cleans your system and reduces stress. When you flush out the day's troubles and hassles, it's like dropping a fifty-pound backpack. You'll be happier and healthier. Regular personal expression with your woman will add years to your life. Do you know why men die, on average, eight years before their wives? Because they want to! Actually, that's not true. Men die earlier, and one major cause is that they hold things in. They stuff emotions and stress and eventually die from the internal damage this lack of expression causes.

In addition to living longer, the real benefit of sharing

personally is a deeper relationship with your wife. You will experience something most men never do: intimacy with a member of the opposite sex. You will create emotional intimacy, and that will flow naturally into physical intimacy.

THE PAD

All of us husbands need some tools to learn how to open up with our wives. One very effective tool is the pad. Buy several writing pads, the small ones you can find in any drug store or stationery store. Keep a pad with you at all times. And a pen. Keep a pad in the car. Keep a pad at your desk. Keep a pad at home.

The pad is for jotting down events and feelings and situations that happen during your day. Right after something happens, jot it down if you think it might interest your wife. It might be a strong emotion like anger, frustration, or joy. It might be a stressful interaction with your boss. It might be a memory of something you and your wife did years ago. These experiences may seem trivial to you; they are not to your wife!

At the end of the day, you have a nice little list of things that happened to you. It's a window into the real you, the inside you, the you your woman longs to get to know. You need the pad because if you don't write down these personal items as they occur, guess what will happen? You will forget them and have nothing to say that evening to your dear, long-suffering wife. She'll ask: "What happened today?" And, like an idiot, you'll reply: "Nothing."

Unfortunately, you will be telling the truth. Most men simply cannot remember anything that happened over thirty minutes ago. Their day is like a giant scroll rolling up after them, blotting out everything that takes place. Even if something dramatic happens, if it's not written down as I suggest, a man will not remember it.

Let's say that the man is eating lunch at a streetside café when suddenly a huge crowd surges past his table. There are sirens, police, and screaming people. He looks up. The pope is riding by in his popemobile. The pontiff actually stops, calls the man over, and whispers to him: "Bless you, my son. Go home and talk to your wife." When this man gets home, his wife asks him: "What happened today?" He'll say, in complete honesty: "Nothing." Because he didn't jot down the meeting with the Pope, it's gone forever.

Women don't need a pad. They remember everything, in minute detail, from their day. They can easily and quite automatically recall every single emotion and event that occurred from the moment they woke up.

When a man gets home, his day is over, and he has no memory of it. He wants to relax and think about what he'll do that evening and the next day. The trouble is, most great conversations are built on what happened that day. Guys, use the pad.

When you get home, help your wife get the kids' needs met, and then go to her and start a conversation. Don't allow her to ask you questions first, or you'll be on the defensive. You may feel controlled. Beat her to the punch! You now have something to say because there are several items on your pad. Holding your pad, tell her what happened to you today. You'll be in control, and she'll be happy because you're sharing with her.

By the way, don't do what one man in a seminar audience told me he wanted to do. He asked: "Dr. Clarke, can't

I just hand her the pad?" I said: "No! *Refer* to the pad, but *talk* to her!"

This pad idea is a winner, believe me, but it will take time and practice to hone this new skill.

Ladies, please be patient as the man learns. The first few times he uses the pad—maybe the first twenty-five or thirty times—his list won't be too impressive. The things he chooses to jot down won't be too deep or personal. "Went to the store and bought batteries." "Got a paper cut and thought to myself: *Wow, that's a bad paper cut!*" Give him time. He'll get better.

Praise him for his efforts. Give him only encouragement for the first month. Then gently—very gently—tell him the kinds of things you'd like him to jot down: emotions, information about people, job stress, his spiritual life, etc. Don't demand. Don't be critical. Don't bring this up during a conversation in which he's using his list. Wait awhile, then in a warm, loving moment tell him what you'd like to hear. You might even write this in a note, because that's not as threatening as in person.

Husbands, that's the first skill you need to master in order to share personally with your woman. Use the pad. It will help. Now, let's take a look at the second critical skill we men need to help us open up.

SIX

MEN WHO FOLLOW,
MEN WHO LEAD

The adult male lion is known throughout the world as the unquestioned king of the animals. What a majestic creature! His huge, regal head is framed by a glorious mane of long, lustrous hair. His ferocious growl sends other animals scampering away in fear. The dominant male leads his pride of lions with courage and decisive action. His awesome authority is unchallenged by the females and other males under his rule. He is a leader to be admired and respected. Or is he?

This is the commonly accepted view of the male lion. Too

bad it's not even close to the truth. Oh, he looks majestic all right. At first glance, it looks like he calls the shots in the pride. The sad truth is the male lion is nothing more than a weak, spineless, and lazy momma's boy. He sleeps the day away. Talk about a couch potato! The only time he gets up is to relieve himself or have sex with one of the females.

In the most important activity of the pride, killing prey for meat, the male allows the females to do all the real work. All he does is roar from the bushes, scaring the targeted animals toward the females. It is the ladies who must chase and kill the prey. The male shows up at the tail end of the hunt and pigs out. What a wimp!

Men, I hate to say this, but most of us are like the male lion in our homes. We don't lead, we follow. We allow the women to do all the work. We show up for meals, and we do approach our mates for sex. That's about it.

BEFORE MARRIAGE, MEN LEAD

The second tool we clams need in order to open up is to initiate. Before marriage, men initiate a great deal. We ask women out. We set up creative, romantic dates. We call her on the phone. We ask them what jobs we can do for them. We even talk to them! We start conversations spontaneously!

This initiating is all part of the pursuit. Men are so decisive, so full of action when there is a desirable goal. All this initiating activity pleases women. It makes them feel cared for and loved. It makes women and men feel closer. And, of course, it leads to marriage.

After Marriage, Men Follow

After marriage, many men stop initiating at home. Once we get the woman, we decide we can relax. Most men take very little action, if any, in household chores, with the children, and in the marriage relationship. We take a backseat. Like the male lion, a man lies around and lets the female do all the work.

Guess who steps into the vacuum and becomes the leader, the initiator in many areas? The woman! Somebody has to do it. She is the foreman and assigns the chores. She makes the decisions regarding the children. She plans dates, if there are any. Ask any lady: "Isn't it fun to plan your own dates and ask him out?" It's pathetic!

The woman handles all the holidays and birthdays. She keeps track of relatives' birthdays! She sends family cards. All the man has to do is sign his name while emitting a roar and tossing a mane regally. The woman buys all the presents! (Half the time the man doesn't even know what presents were bought for the family.) The woman plans vacations and packs for them. When the car is all ready, the man comes out to the car and gets to drive. He has to have control. I say, "No! You don't pack, you don't drive!"

Men say: "I work hard all day and make decisions, and I just want to relax at home." It's a big fat cop out. I know, because I used that line on Sandy for years.

God says men are to be the leaders in their homes. Read Ephesians 5:22–23 (NAS): "Wives, be subject to your own husbands, as to the Lord. For the husband is the head of the wife. . ." That's leadership. Leadership means stepping forward and being out front, not bringing up the rear. God doesn't care if a male lion is a leader or a follower. He does care if a husband is a leader or a follower.

Men, when you fail to initiate, you set the woman up as the leader and the initiator. That puts you in the responding position, in the position of follower. This is not what God wants, and it won't work. And when you do this, you are automatically on the defensive. You are being told what to do, and you don't like it. You feel controlled. That makes you angry and frustrated. But you have set yourself up. It's your own fault! Not only is it wrong for you, but it is not right or fair for your wife.

INITIATE MORE AT HOME

There is a way out of this uncomfortable and, frankly, un-biblical role. Start initiating at home. Take an active role as the leader. Using the pad and beginning conversations are one way to initiate. There are others.

Do things before you have to be asked by the woman. When you act on your own, you elimi-nate your feeling of being controlled.

Set up a schedule of regular daily and weekly chores that are your responsibility. Make sure you do your fair share. Write them down, post them, and do them without the woman saying a word. If you stall and she has to remind you, you've blown it.

Every day, several times a day, ask your woman what jobs need to be done. Even if you do your regular household chores, all kinds of errands and jobs pop up daily. When she gives you a list of jobs in response to your question, jot down the ones you agree to do and do them.

If you have children, be an active father. Change diapers, help with homework, discipline them, give baths, tuck them in, and lead family devotions once a week. ("And, fathers, do not provoke your children to anger; but bring them up in the discipline and instruction of the Lord" [Ephesians 6:4, NAS].) This is the kind of dad your wife and kids need.

Picture this scene. You arrive home from work, kiss your wife on the lips (not on the cheek or forehead), and ask her what you can do to help her. After nearly fainting from shock, she mentions a few things you can do. You do the few extra jobs she's given you, help with the kids, and finish your regular chores.

When the kids are in their bedroom or confined to another part of the house, you actually invite her to sit down for a time of communication. She looks at you strangely. She asks if you're feeling okay, but she accepts your invitation. Using your pad and notes, begin the conversation by sharing with her some interesting things that happened to you today.

Your woman will love this. She'll love you. She'll feel loved and cherished. You'll like the good vibes coming back from her, believe me. It's going to be a great night because you have initiated. You have led the way! This is male leadership. (Actually, you can have a lot of great nights if you follow these steps.) Can you imagine how much better your relationship will be if you initiate like this every day? Hey, doing it even three or four times a week will make a difference. Try it, and you'll see.

When you initiate, you lighten your busy wife's load. Women were not designed to be the primary initiators, and it wears on them. Your woman will have more energy, and some of that energy can be spent meeting your needs. When you initiate, your woman feels closer to you, and you are in control in a healthy way. You'll get her out of the Big Momma, parental, "I'm in charge" role, and back into the soft, warm, "I'm your woman" role. And she will respect you again. She will be able to love you in a deeper, more romantic way. She will be much more interested in physical touch and sex.

Most of all, God is pleased and will honor you for obeying His instructions in the Bible.

SEVEN

WOMEN, DROP YOUR CROWBARS!

M ale bashing is a popular sport, in secular culture and in the Christian community. Men are jerks. Men are slobs. Men are selfish. Men are insensitive. Men are, well, Neanderthals who simply don't have the relational tools to really connect with a woman.

American culture's view of men has changed dramatically over the past thirty years. This change is perhaps most clearly seen in the medium of television. In the 1960s and 1970s, television husbands and fathers were stable, kind, and loving. We could look up to and admire men like Ward

Cleaver and Mike Brady. In the 1980s and 1990s, we've been treated to such paragons of virtue as J. R. Ewing and Pee Wee Herman. Quite a change, wouldn't you say?

Television movies and talk shows bring us a never-ending parade of wife batterers, alcoholics, serial killers, child abusers, and adulterers. Best-selling books attract women readers by the millions with titles like, "Men Who (fill in the blank with some horrible lifestyle or crime), and the Women Who (love/tolerate/put up with them)."

Enough, already. Where are all the normal men? Where are all the real men? Most of us are just regular guys. We're not all a bunch of twisted, evil deviants who enjoy destroying the lives of women. We're not perfect, but we don't kill people or abuse our wives. The truth is, most of us love our wives and want to have good marriages.

If it were just our culture trashing men, it wouldn't be so bad. Actually, it would be perfectly understandable. Portrayals of mean, rotten men raise ratings and sell books. The problem is, this low view of men has seeped into the evangelical community.

Too many Christian books, radio shows, and marriage seminars identify men as the problem in the marriage relationship. Men are often raked over the coals for their shortcomings, while the women get off with hardly a slap on the wrist. This unbalanced approach is not fair, is not accurate, and needs to be corrected. And I'm just the guy to do it!

It's easy to blame the man for marital problems. His mistakes are obvious. He won't allow closeness and resists the woman's attempts to achieve intimacy. He won't talk. He won't be romantic. He won't come home on time from work. He won't. He won't. He won't. It's true. He won't.

Without question, most men have these weaknesses.

Men have their faults, and I'm hard on men in my therapy office and in my seminars. We men, as God's chosen leaders in our marriages, need to work hard on our relationship skills. Men *are* half of the problem in their marriages. Guess who is the other half? That's right, for every clam, there is a crowbar. I'm pretty hard on women, too, because they feed into marital problems just as much as the men.

Ladies, you have your own set of relationship weaknesses. You are doing things—or not doing things—every day that actually prevent the very intimacy you so desperately want and need.

That's right. I'm talking directly to you ladies in this chapter. All of you crowbars have some serious work to do. You need to see what you are doing wrong and correct it. When you fix your half of the problems, that's all you can do. The rest is up to the men. But believe me, as you change in the key areas I am about to describe, there is a good chance you can motivate your clam to do some healthy changing, too.

STOP TRYING SO HARD

Many of you make the mistake of escalating, getting too intense in your efforts to open up the clam. You are determined to get into that clam. After all, it's not just for you. It's also in the best interest of the clam. If he stays shut, there is no closeness, and he slowly dies in there. So, like Joan of Arc, you swear a blood oath to save the day. You'll beat on that clam and beat on that clam until one day, one beautiful day, he'll open up, and all nature will rejoice. (You may recall that Joan of Arc, despite her passion and will to win, burned at the stake.) If you attack the clam head on, you will go up in flames just like poor old Joan.

Listen to me. My dear Crowbars, if you push too hard, three things happen. And they're all bad.

First, you hit his control alarm and, true to his clam nature, he closes up even tighter. You actually make it more difficult for him to respond. He will instinctively shut down. If he knows you really, really want closeness, he'll stiffen up all the more. He sees it as a contest, a power struggle, in which he feels he has something to lose. And he intends to win.

Ladies, think about it. How many times have you gone to the man with a very important request, only to be turned down cold? Maybe you were crying. Maybe you were literally shaking with rage. Maybe your voice was raised. With a man, the sad truth is, the more you want something the less chance you'll get it. Crazy, isn't it?

If you don't give up, but continue to try to get what you want, he continues to deny you. But if you do give up, throw away your crowbar, and accept that it's not going to happen, something amazing takes place. What happens? The man, released from his control mode, will often come back to you and give you what you wanted!

The second bad thing that happens is that your intensity becomes the issue. You are asking for closeness. That's a perfectly reasonable and important request. But if you ask with too much intensity, your desire for closeness is completely lost in the transaction. Believe me, closeness is the last thing on the man's mind as the crowbar bangs against his clamshell. He is under siege! "May Day! May Day! This lady is trying to kill me! Or worse, she's trying to control me." He's not even aware of why you're so intense, just that you are intense.

As you pepper him with questions or urge him to talk to you, he is thinking a number of unflattering thoughts. "I gotta get out of here." "How can I get this screaming meemie off me?" "Wow, she is way too angry!" "What a nag!" "She's way out of line!" "She's out of control!" "How dare she use that tone with me!" He won't express these thoughts to you, but he's thinking them.

I know what men think inside because—besides being a man—when working with them in marriage therapy sessions, I can get men to tell me what they are thinking. How?

Often, I'll have the woman do her usual crowbar routine. Then, after a few minutes, I'll ask the man what's going on in his head. The wife is very often shocked to hear the defensive internal dialogue going on in her husband's mind. She doesn't realize how intense the man perceives her to be, and how massively turned off he instantly becomes.

Third, ladies, when you press too hard you suffer damage personally. You become increasingly more resentful, depressed, and hurt. Your self-esteem and confidence drain away. Because you want closeness with your man so badly, it's easy to make it the focus of your life. While understandable, this is a big mistake.

I've talked to many women who have been broken by constantly throwing themselves against the clam. They have made getting the man to open up their number one goal. It is often their only goal in life. Their frustration, bitterness, and stress level are through the roof. The result is a variety of debilitating psychological and physical problems.

Part of my job as a psychologist is to convince these crowbars that there is more to life than their single-minded pursuit of an open clam. I tell them they are creating a triple whammy. First, their intense approach is doomed to fail.

Second, if this is their number one goal in life then they will experience continual failure because they'll never reach it. Third, they will suffer the same psychological and physical problems of battle-weary veterans of a losing war.

Ladies, please believe me when I tell you there is nothing specific you can do to open your clam. Any direct approach with a man is doomed to fail. Unless you enjoy being a martyr and wasting your life, drop your crowbar, and back. . . away. . .slowly.

Control will always be inside a man—always. You can't get rid of it. It is a God-given trait in all men. You have to learn how to deal with it in subtle, indirect ways. Let me show you how to do this.

Pull Back from the Man

You are too close to the man, and it's time to create a little space. What do you do when someone gets too physically close to you in a conversation? The person is invading your personal space. You can feel her breath and know exactly what she had for lunch. When this happens, you back away to a comfortable distance, don't you?

The same thing happens when you get too emotionally close to the man. You are invading the man's personal airspace, swinging your crowbar, and so he naturally moves away from you. You need to be the one to move. You don't pull back too far. You don't ignore him. You don't leave the relationship. You move away just enough to give you and him some room to maneuver.

GET A LIFE

Your man ought to be a part of your life, but not all of it. Even if this clam does learn how to open up for you, you still need a life of your own. He can't meet all your needs on his best day. In a best-case scenario, a loving and attentive husband can meet only 30 percent of your minimum daily need requirements. That leaves 70 percent you have to get fulfilled from a variety of other sources.

Develop and nurture your personal relationship with God. God certainly ought to be the biggest "hose" coming into your need tank. If you don't know God personally, the first step is establishing the relationship through faith in His Son, Jesus Christ.

There is only one God, and that's the God of the Bible. There's only one way to reach God, and that's through Jesus. If you believe that Jesus Christ died on the cross for your sins (all the bad things you have done) and rose from the dead, you are a Christian. You know God.

Once you know God, you need to grow in the relationship. The closer you get to God, the more power and peace and joy you will have in your life. Spend time with God daily, praying and reading the Bible. Pray to Him throughout the day. Open your eyes and see how He guides your every step each day. Make church attendance and meeting with fellow Christians a vital part of your life.

As critically important as God is to your needs and happiness, you must develop other need sources. Every lady reading these words must—I said must—have at least one close female friend. I'm talking about a kindred spirit, a real buddy, a best friend. Someone with whom you can share your heart: your triumphs, your tragedies, your life with

God, your marriage, your children, your hopes, and your dreams. Someone with whom you can laugh and cry and be totally yourself.

You must develop a life outside your home. This could mean a paying job, volunteer activities, church involvement, a hobby, or some combination of all of these. Don't make the mistake of putting all your eggs in the basket of home. Home and marriage and family are important, but they are not enough to fill your need tank. So, get out there and get a life!

Also, ladies, you simply have to stick to a regular exercise program. Of course, so do the men. The energy and vitality you require to perform all your daily jobs will come, in part, from exercise. What you need to do is thirty minutes of moderate exercise, three times a week. That's all. You don't have to train like a triathlete to be in great physical shape.

This pulling back from the man and developing your own need sources pays off big-time in three ways.

First, it's good for you, which is the main point. You'll be happier and more fulfilled because you're getting your needs met. You'll also experience the wonderful feeling of God using you in His service.

Second, this personal development will help you live with your clam. It's not easy living with a clam. As your life expands, you'll have the energy and the patience to put up with that clam. When he shuts you out, it will still hurt, but you'll have the resources to counteract the pain. It will sting, but it won't ruin your day and drag you down.

Third, your individual enrichment is good for your
   man. It lessens the pressure he feels to meet
   your needs. It creates a more comfortable space
   between him and you. Knowing he doesn't have
   to meet all your needs actually frees the man to
   do more for you. Your personal growth won't
   threaten him. Instead, it will, very possibly,
   motivate him to come your way. When a man
   realizes he doesn't have to do something, he's
   much more likely to do it.

EIGHT

WORK LESS, TALK LESS, PRAISE MORE

I t's pretty tough to build your own life if you are doing 90 percent of the household chores. You'll not only resent the man, but you'll be physically and emotionally drained. I've counseled many women who simply don't have the time or the energy to get out of the house and develop a life. They feel they have to do most of the chores. I mean, if the man won't do his fair share, what can you do?

STOP DOING ALL THE CHORES

I'll tell you what you can do. You can stop doing the jobs that you believe the man ought to be doing. You're not mean about it. You're not nasty about it. There are no dramatic scenes or hysterics. You simply tell him that you will no longer be responsible for these jobs, and you list them for him.

Let's face it. If the man knows you'll eventually knuckle under and do these jobs, he'll be happy to let you do it. So, you're not bluffing. This time, you mean it. It's not some massive challenge or emotional showdown. In fact, the less emotion you show the better. That way, he'll know you're serious.

Early in our marriage, Sandy did everything around the apartment. (Hey, I was an important seminary student. I had to study a lot. I was preparing for my career.) One day, Sandy informed me she had had enough and told me the jobs I needed to do. After my initial shock and anger, I got to work. I found that almost immediately Sandy was happier and had more energy and time to meet her own needs and mine.

Here's how: Tell your husband you're sorry for creating a monster. For years, because you did most of the work, you trained him to not do it. It's called enabling. But now it's over. Tell him it may take him awhile to adjust to this new program, and you hope he can. You're rooting for him. You have decided that even though the adjustment will be diffi-cult, it will be worth the pain. You won't continue in slavery because it is breaking you down physically, emotionally, and spiritually. Not only can you not build a life of your own, you can't be a good wife to him. You are (like my Sandy used to be) too tired, and too busy, and too resentful.

Let's assume your husband resists this new role and

takes awhile to get into the harness. If your kids are old enough (school age), put them to work. If you can afford it, hire a housekeeper to come in once a week to do the jobs he ought to be doing. Some husbands have no shame and will allow the kids or a housekeeper to do their jobs. So be it. You're still better off because you're not killing yourself doing the jobs.

What do you do with a man who promises to take care of household projects but stalls and doesn't follow through? Don't bother nagging him. That'll just increase his resistance. Simply give him a reasonable time frame to complete the job. If he fails to meet the deadline, hire someone to do it or find a friend to help. If this embarrasses him, tough! It was his choice.

I saw a married woman in therapy some time ago who complained that her husband refused to mow the lawn. The grass got higher and higher, and she was tearing her hair out. I told her to relax because the neighbors would blame the man of the house, not her. I recommended she put up a big sign in her front yard that read: HUSBAND WON'T MOW LAWN. I told her to not mow that lawn no matter how high it got.

As I recall, she didn't use the sign idea. She hired a boy down the street to mow it. Eventually, her husband decided to mow regularly to save the money. I think he was embarrassed, but whatever the reason, he came around.

STOP TALKING SO MUCH

Ladies, let me guess. You start 98 percent of the conversations with your husband, don't you? You talk about your day. You describe the events in your life. You share your emotions. If he doesn't react to what you share, you ask him questions.

How is this approach working? Is your man responding by talking about his own life and sharing his emotions? I doubt it. When you begin virtually all the conversations, you are being a crowbar. He'll get defensive and won't talk.

It's time to try something different. Stop starting all the conversations. You can start some—even 50 or 60 percent—but not all of them. Be quieter with the man. Get comfortable with silence. He might just start some conversations on his own. Maybe he'll talk to you about your day. Maybe he'll ask what you're thinking, how you're feeling. Wouldn't that be a nice switch?

If he asks you why you're quieter, tell him: "Honey, I'm just a little tired of always starting our talks. I think maybe I've been monopolizing our conversations and want to give you a chance. It may take awhile, but I'd like you to try talking first, at least part of the time."

Not only do you start too many conversations, you also carry too many conversations. How can I say this delicately, with sensitivity? You talk too much. You fill the air with words and overwhelm the man's weak listening apparatus. He tunes out, you catch him, and you're angry and hurt. The conversation is over. And if he doesn't tune you out and is actually listening, it won't make any difference. The more words you use, the higher his resistance to talking. He can't compete with your impressive verbiage, so he won't even try. Plus, he can't get a word in edgewise in the face of your avalanche of sentences.

This won't be easy, but reduce your volume of words. Try a technique that has helped many of my therapy couples: the ten-minute rule. Talk for ten minutes and then take a break. At this point, it's the man's turn to talk. He could respond to what you've said or share his own personal stuff. Or, he may have nothing to say at the ten-minute mark. That's a distinct possibility. If that happens, let some silence go by. Give him a chance to respond, to say something. As you'll see in an upcoming chapter, men need time to process. If he still has nothing to say, let more silence go by, or talk about something else for ten minutes.

CHANGE YOUR
CONVERSATIONAL STYLE

In order to avoid triggering the man's control mechanism, you must learn to approach him in a different way. A fundamental shift in your conversational style is required. If you can admit the way you're doing it now isn't working, give my way a try.

ONE-WAY COMMUNICATION

First, when you want something from the man you need to learn to ask with one-way communication. You might want help with the kids, help with the chores, his attention, his time, or for him to open up and share something personal. Whatever you want or need, you must ask him directly in a low-intensity, concise way with no expectation of a response.

The idea here is to send your request in a manner most likely to be heard and considered by the man. So, make it brief. Keep your emotions in check and your intensity as low as possible. Above all, do not ask or expect him to respond. This is not a dialogue. Simply deliver your message, and drop the subject. Let silence go by, change the subject, or walk away. You won't bring it up again. He will have to come to you with a response, if he has one.

You're thinking: *How can I keep my emotions in check and my intensity low? I'm a woman! Emotional intensity is what I do!* I know, I know. I'm not suggesting that you become an emotional robot. Just work to keep your intensity lower than usual. You're still going to be intense, but if it's beneath the man's threshold, you're okay.

Ask the man to work with you as you practice. Admit to him that you know your intensity turns him off, and you're trying to come to him in a different way. Ask him to tell you if you're being too intense when you make a request. With practice, you'll learn just how intense you can be without shutting him down.

Here's an example of what a wife might say to her husband, using my approach. She sits down next to him in the den and says: "Honey, these past few weeks you've been very busy at work. All those late hours must be tough. I miss you and want some time with you. I'd like you to carve out some time to talk the next few evenings, and take me out Saturday evening. It's up to you. Think about it." Then, she gets up and walks out of the room.

This lady has done the best she could do in one-way communication. She expressed a need honestly and briefly, but without intensity. There's at least a chance he'll respond because he heard the message in an unpressured, nondefensive way. She left the ball in his court, which gives him the control he needs. She'll do nothing to manipulate or force him to respond. It's up to him.

WRITE THE MAN

Another effective one-way communication tool is writing a short note to the man. Usually, you will ask him for something verbally, but sometimes a note is helpful if it's a very important issue. You can say exactly what you want without fear of intensity because the communication is in print, not in person. The man's control is not threatened because it's just him and the letter. Chances are good he'll take in your message and think about it. As with verbal one-way communication, you do not press him for a response.

It's possible the man may never even mention getting your note. You must bite your tongue and not ask the pathetic, classic crowbar question: "Did you read my note?"

CLEAN YOUR SYSTEM

The final one-way communication method is the periodic expression of your feelings when the man does not open up and meet your need for closeness. When the man angers, hurts, or disappoints you, these painful feelings must be expressed and released. Not to get a reaction, but to clean your system and avoid the buildup of bitterness.

The same one-way rules apply. In person or in a letter, briefly share your pain with the man. Make it clear he does not have to respond. Do this every several weeks or when you notice your pain is impacting you personally, spiritually, or in the relationship.

Here's an example of a note written by a wife who needed to clean her system:

Dear Bob:

There are some things I need to get off my chest. Over the past month, I have felt you've been very distant and critical.

I have tried to get you to talk about what's bothering you, but you've refused. I guess I've been a nag, and I'm sorry for that. I'm angry and hurt because you've shut me out.

When and if you're ready to tell me what's going on, I'll be here.

You don't need to respond to this note. I needed to express my feelings so I don't become bitter and resentful.

Love, Betty

This pulling back from the man and using one-way communication is good for you and might just get the man's attention. If you pursue him, as many women mistakenly do, you will never succeed in achieving closeness. He'll run away every time. If, however, he gets back to pursuing you, now we're talking!

Make yourself—not a challenge to get away from and resist, but—someone to win back. Maybe—just maybe—you can get the man back into the pursuit mode. Men *need* to pursue. It's an innate drive. And women need to be pursued. So back off, and let's see if your clam will come after you.

LEARN TO PRAISE YOUR MAN

Ladies, I don't want you to think I'm suggesting you back off in every area of the relationship. I'm not suggesting that at all. You still start your share of conversations, you still meet needs, and you still express love for your man. Praising him is one of the most powerful ways to love a man. And it is one of the secrets to opening a clam. Your clam still has to choose to open, but he's going to want to when he's showered with praise. That's right, ladies, I said showered. As in, do it a lot. A little token praise won't cut it. It's like being given two bites of a fabulous filet mignon, and then having the plate whisked away. That's cruel.

Men need to be praised, especially by their women. It's not just nice. It's not just an extra. We need it from you. Women praise us in courtship then drop it after marriage. There goes the filet mignon.

Men need praise because we just like the attention and the satisfaction for doing a good job. A pat on the back feels good. We like credit for doing things. That may be petty, but it's the truth. (It's a guy thing, okay? We are externally motivated.) We also need praise because women are confusing to us, and it's difficult to figure out what makes them happy. We need feedback in the form of praise for behavior that pleases.

If I do a job for Sandy and she says nothing about it, I have two reactions. I'm hurt and angry because I didn't get praised. I also think the job didn't mean that much to her. If Sandy wants to keep me initiating and helping, she needs to praise me. It's still my responsibility to do these things for her, but praise makes it a lot easier.

Many women have trouble praising their men, especially for small jobs. Women think: *That's a drop in the bucket compared to what I do.* True, but that's not the point. The point is, ladies, it's smart to develop the habit of praising your man when he does something that you like. You are teaching him how to love you, how to meet your needs. Don't assume he knows you're pleased with a behavior. Tell him! Make him feel as though he did something good!

He'll keep doing the behaviors you praise, and he'll do more, hoping for more praise. He'll feel loved. He'll feel closer to you. Now, here's the good part: The clam will open up more easily! When a man is bathed in praise, he feels so good and so confident and so in control that he is able to open up and let you in.

Now, don't gush all over him and make a huge fuss. That isn't necessary. Ask him what kind of praise and positive reinforcement he wants. Let him define praise. It could be a few words. It could be a touch. It could be food. Find out what he wants and give it to him often. It's a small price to pay for the real possibility of motivating your clam to open.

NINE

IT'S ALL IN YOUR MIND, SWEETHEART

A man and a woman are in conversation. It's just the two of them. At first, everything's fine. There's eye contact and a comfortable feeling of closeness. Both are taking turns talking and listening. Then suddenly, it happens. The woman notices that the man is not listening. She sees all the telltale signs. His mouth is hanging open, and a small line of spittle is running down his chin. His eyes are glassy and staring off into the distance. His body is rigid. There's not even a twitch.

Is it a stroke? Could it be some kind of a seizure? Have aliens invaded his body? No. It's what all women hate. It's what drives them crazy. It's the *zone*.

THE MALE ZONE

The zone is a periodic mental blank spot that men move into without warning. During the zone, there appears to be very little, if any, brain activity. For a brief period, conscious thought ceases. The man is, for all intents and purposes, a vegetable.

The woman takes the zone personally and says: "You're not listening to me!" She's right. He's not. Now, it's bad enough at this point. The woman is insulted and angry because the man wasn't paying attention to her. But it gets worse. The woman, being a woman, has to ask this question: "What were you thinking about?" The man, being a man, with all sincerity has to respond: "Nothing." The woman can't believe it. "What do you mean, nothing?" She can't conceive of going blank and having nothing on her mind. It's never happened to her. She's convinced he's lying. He had to be thinking of something!

Men, if we could just come up with something that we were thinking, it might help satisfy the woman. At the least, it would be some damage control.

"I was thinking of a cure for cancer just now."

"I was thinking of some way to achieve world
    peace."

"Honey, funny you should ask. I was just thinking
    of how beautiful you are, my darling."

Oh, if we could tell her something, anything at all, that

we were thinking! But we can't! We have to admit the sad, pitiful truth. We had absolutely nothing in the brain.

Speaking on behalf of all men, ladies, let me assure you that the zone is not an intentional attempt to drive you over the edge of sanity. It just seems that way. It's a perfectly natural, normal part of being a man. The male zone is just one minor example of a very important truth. Men and women think differently. Our brains are different, and so the way we think, the way we talk, and the way we process personal information is different. And these differences block us in conversation.

In the next several chapters, we'll take a look at some key thinking differences between men and women. I'll show you how these differences affect opposite-sex conversations. Most importantly, I'll teach you how to adjust to these differences to achieve real depth in your conversations, because if you can have great conversations, you can have a great marriage!

"What Did the Movie Mean to You?"

Picture this scene. A man and a woman have just seen a movie together and are walking out of the theater. The movie was a powerful, touching drama—a love story in which a family member died and there were many emotionally intense scenes. The hero and the heroine almost lost each other, but in the end were reunited. It was pretty heavy stuff. The kind of movie women love.

The woman, who is crying, spends the next ten minutes sharing her reaction to the movie. She covers, in detail, what she liked about it, what she didn't like, her emotions, events in her own life that the movie reminded her of, how the movie related to her relationship with the man, etcetera, etcetera, etcetera. They're in the car halfway to the restaurant when she finishes. She asks the man: "What did you think of the movie?" He replies: "Oh, I liked it okay." That's it. He stops. That's all he says.

How many women would be satisfied with that response? None! This poor lady is like a desert that has just gotten one drop of rain. She wants more! But chances are good she isn't going to get any more. At least, not right then. She can begin asking questions, probing, trying to get at what's inside the man. But what's going to happen? She won't get too far. In fact, nowhere at all. The man will feel pressured and controlled. He'll clam up tight.

This scene illustrates a key difference between men and women. Women are external, relational processors. Men are internal, solitary processors. To learn how to communicate as a couple, you must understand this difference. Let me describe the four areas that make up these two styles of processing.

WOMEN ARE IN TOUCH, MEN ARE OUT OF TOUCH

Women are in constant touch with their personal, inside information: thoughts, feelings, reactions, pain, hopes, and dreams. Women know what's inside at all times. It's all just right there at the surface. It's automatic. It's instantaneous. When an event occurs, a woman reacts, and she knows what her reaction is.

Men are not in touch with their personal, inside stuff. The good news is, men do react to events with thoughts, emotions, pain, and other personal information. The bad news is, they have no idea what their reactions are. Their personal responses are deep inside, and it takes time to locate them.

Our movie man does have a reaction to the movie, unless he's a complete stick. But he doesn't know what it is yet. He really doesn't. He'll have to look for it.

Women Share, Men Suppress

Women not only know what's inside, they naturally and spontaneously share it. It comes up and out. "I know what I'm thinking and feeling, and I'm going to tell you right now." They've been doing this their whole lives! Women can't stand to hold in what's inside. They have to get it out as soon as possible.

Men naturally and spontaneously suppress their personal information. It stays inside where no one can see it. We don't show it to anyone. We've been taught to suppress it. The act of stuffing our feelings and reactions is an automatic reflex. We don't even realize we're doing it most of the time.

Women Relate, Men Retreat

Women share with another person. For a woman, an event hasn't happened until she shares it. She'll find someone, believe me. Just check your phone bill! She'll talk to her mother, her sister, a friend, a neighbor, and anyone else who will listen.

Did you ever notice how a woman will tell the same story to a number of people? Once or twice is never enough.

Oh, no. She'll call eight persons and describe the same event, adding details and extra information each time. She never seems to get tired of telling this same story. She enjoys the act of relating the story because she is sharing herself. It is her way of saying, "I love you and want to be close to you. Here is a piece of who I am. You can see what I'm like inside by how I acted and felt and responded in this event today."

She'll also tell her husband, whether he wants to hear it or not. She wants and needs her husband to relive the event with her as she tells it. (Husband: Don't just sit there and gut your way through the story. She's giving you the gift of herself and, to receive it and connect with her, you must be an active listener.) React as she's talking. Laugh in the right places. Feel pain and disappointment if that's what she's feeling.

There's a good reason why men seem unable to be active listeners. By nature, we retreat with our personal information. Men are programmed to withdraw and process what's inside, alone. We don't run and find a person to talk to about our feelings and internal reactions to events. Are you kidding? If we process at all, we do it totally and completely alone.

Since a man is extremely uncomfortable sharing what's inside, he tends to be just as uncomfortable when his woman shares her insides. The typical man is blown away by the typical woman's spontaneous, incredibly detailed, and emotional description of an event in her life. He doesn't see the need to talk out inside stuff. He doesn't understand that she is sharing herself and looking for a love connection.

WOMEN WING IT,
MEN MULL IT OVER

Women process as they talk. They make connections and figure out their reactions as they go. When a woman begins talking, she has no idea where she'll end up, and she doesn't care. Very often, a woman will start a conversation this way: "I don't know how I feel, but. . ." She'll pull the whole thing together somehow. Of course the man is thinking: *Well, if you don't know, be quiet. Let me know when you've figured it all out.* He wants the short, condensed version and not the long, drawn-out one.

Here's an example using our movie lady. As she walks out of the theater, she says:

"Oh, honey, that movie touched me. Wow, I have so many different feelings it's hard to sort them all out. You know that part where the long grass in the valley was blowing in the wind? That reminds me of the blue grass of Kentucky, and all the horses running free. I love horses. My grandma had a farm when I was small. She had a pony named Bumpers and, oh, how I loved that pony! The pony died one winter of uncontrollable diarrhea, and I was crushed. I cried and cried and. . ."

The man is thinking: *What is she talking about? What do Kentucky, her grandma, and the death of a pony named Bumpers from diarrhea have to do with that movie?* He's completely lost as she bounces from one topic to another. She's a conversational pinball! And she's just getting started. She's expressing whatever comes into her head and enjoying every minute of it. She'll eventually sift through all her feelings and wind up her monologue, but it may be awhile.

Men do all their processing internally. It's a big secret.

Before a man will share verbally what's inside, he'll go through a careful series of steps. He first has to find out what's there. Then, he'll chew on it. He'll mull it over. He'll think it all through twenty times. He'll organize it and collate it. Finally, he has his response all figured out and put into concise and presentable form. Then, he may—just may—decide to give it to the woman.

A man won't wing it. You won't ever hear a man say, "Well, honey, I'm not sure what I'm feeling, but here goes." No way. He'll go through his painstaking mental inventory every time. He has to. He's a man. He won't blurt out something that might embarrass him. When he speaks, he knows what he's going to say. A little short on spontaneity, and long on control.

Here's an illustration of these two different styles of communication that I often use in my marriage workshops. There are two artists, one female and one male. The way they work is a reflection of how women and men act in conversation.

The female artist has a studio right in the middle of town. There's a big sign out front with her name on it. When she's ready to create a painting, she calls all her friends and invites them to her studio.

Ten or twelve friends come and sit in folding chairs in front of a large blank canvas. When all are seated, the artist begins her painting. With the small audience watching, she brushes paint on the canvas and shapes it. She talks to her friends as she paints, telling them what she's doing and why. She invites their comments and reactions. She shares the experience with these persons. In fact, their presence and feedback are a vital part of her creative process. She would be unable to produce a painting without this dynamic dialogue and interaction.

The male artist has a studio, but no one knows where it is. It's located off the beaten path in a deserted part of town. There's no sign out front. When he's ready to create a painting, he calls no one. He sneaks to his studio alone, in the dead of night. He works on his canvas in private, carefully molding his colors and strokes into a finished product. He takes as long as he needs to get it right. He asks for no feedback of any kind because he wants to do it by himself. It's important to him that his painting be his and his alone.

When he is done, he seeks out one person whom he trusts. There will be no audience, no public exhibition of his work. It will be a private showing to one special person. It is hard for him to share his painting with even this one close companion, but he values her opinion. Deep down, he wants and needs to share his work with her.

Back to the movie example to drive my point home. The woman, like this female artist, can't wait to share what's inside. She is aware of her reaction to the movie. She launches into her personal reaction right away, processing as she goes. She could care less if it isn't organized or logical. She just wants to get it out.

The man, like the male artist, needs time and space to process what's inside. The woman thinks he already knows his reaction, just as she knows hers, and is holding out on her. She thinks: *Hey, he was sitting there next to me, wasn't he? He knows what's in there!* No, it's not true; he has no idea what his reaction is yet. He has to look for it. If he does have some idea of what he's feeling about the movie, he's certainly not ready to share it yet. He has to organize it and make it suitable for presentation.

How do a man and a woman connect in conversation when this huge difference in communication styles looms between them? I have an idea—a really nifty one if I do say so myself—for working with this difference. It's going to help you. I call this idea, this illustration, *the train*.

TEN

"THE TRAIN"

Just about every great old romantic movie has a train scene. Think about it. In *North by Northwest,* the Hitchcock thriller, Cary Grant meets the cool, sophisticated Eva Marie Saint on a train. In the climax to *The Music Man,* that timeless musical, Robert Preston misses his train to be with the lovely librarian, Shirley Jones. The sparks fly between Ingrid Bergman and Gregory Peck on a train in *Spellbound.*

Even in the classic of all classic romantic movies, *Casablanca,* a train scene is a pivotal part of the story. Everybody knows about the famous plane scene at the end, but there's a heartbreaking train episode earlier in the movie. Humphrey

Bogart is stiffed big-time by his sweetheart, Ingrid Bergman, at the Paris train station. She never shows up. I'm not sure who's more hurt and outraged, me or Bogie. I haven't forgiven Ingrid yet.

Trains are the very backbone of *While You Were Sleeping*, a modern romantic classic starring Sandra Bullock. The lonely Sandra works at a Chicago Transit Authority train station. She sells a token every day to the dashing man she thinks she loves. Every day he takes the token, smiles, and rides the train away from her little, forlorn token booth. He doesn't even know she exists. At the end of the movie, Sandra takes a train on her honeymoon with the man she really loves. Great stuff!

Now that I have established the key role of the train in all these on-screen love relationships, what's my point? I'll tell you. The train is not just a romantic vehicle for Hollywood stars and their make-believe relationships. Crazy as it may seem, the train can also play a key role in improving the communication of couples today. The train may have done Bogie dirty, but it's going to help you and your partner create closeness in your conversations.

A MAN MUST HAVE HIS TRAIN

Get your imagination warmed up. Picture, in your mind's eye, a train station and a train in front of the station. You can see the station house, the wooden platform, and the long, dark line of cars. Smoke is billowing from the locomotive's engine. A man and a woman are standing on the platform of the station talking as the train prepares to leave. This time, it's not Bogie and Bergman standing in front of the train. It's you and your partner. If you want to pretend that you look like a couple of movie stars, go ahead.

When the man feels the need to get some space and do some processing, he'll get on the train and go down the tracks some distance, alone. (The woman cannot board the train with him.) The trigger for the man boarding the train will be one of two things. One, if he's asked to share personally by the woman. Or two, if on his own (miracles do sometimes happen), he realizes the need to share personally. If he has to share something from inside himself, something below the superficial surface of chitchat, he'll need to get on that train.

He'll use the time on the train to look inside and see what's there. He'll figure out his feelings and personal reaction. He'll pull it all together into some kind of organized package he can understand. Then, when he's ready, he'll come back to the station, find the woman, and start sharing what he's found out.

Now, this is an ideal picture. I can hear the women:

"He'll get on the train all right—to escape me!"

"He won't look inside when he's gone."

"He certainly won't come back to talk."

"Who do you think you're kidding, Dr. Clarke?"

Hang on, ladies. I'll address these concerns. They're all valid, I know.

What you need to understand now is that the man needs the train because he will not, he cannot, stand with the woman and process his inside stuff on the spot. This isn't a cop-out. He literally can't do it. God did not make him that way.

Your typical man has a delayed reaction to anything personal. He can talk spontaneously about sports, the weather, what power tools he'll use to fix the garage door, and what he wants for dinner. If the conversation gets any deeper, he's way out of his element and will clam up. At least temporarily, he becomes the great Sphinx of Egypt. No emotion. No expression. And, of course, no words.

If you try to force a reaction and get something out of him, ladies, you know what will happen. He'll never, and I mean never, give you the personal stuff you really want. He won't give you the satisfaction. That's the way he saves face and maintains control.

You say: "He just won't talk to me!" That's right, he won't. Not when you back him into a conversational corner. You've got to give him some space and time to process, to catch up with you in the personal information department. You've got to give him the right and the freedom to use the train.

The typical woman doesn't need the train. She can talk at the drop of a hat. She's ready to process out loud all the time and usually does. Her problem is reducing the amount of processing so she doesn't bury the man in an avalanche of words.

Ladies, I hate to repeat myself, but I'm going to anyway. You can't expect your man to spontaneously share what's inside. You have a right to expect him to share personally with you. Without mutual sharing, your relationship can't be deep and intimate. What I'm saying is you have to let him do his personal sharing his way. And his way is using the train.

Before he gets on the train, feel free to express yourself fully. Give details, tell your story, share your opinion, and express your emotions. It's also okay to ask the man questions, as long as you're low-key and don't expect immediate answers. Just ask a few questions. Don't pump him—you're not Barbara Walters! That's being a crowbar, and you know where that gets you.

When the man uses the train, it doesn't always mean he leaves physically. This would be rather awkward. "Sorry, honey, gotta go." If you're in a restaurant and he needs the train, he won't excuse himself and go to the bathroom. If you're in the car, he won't pull over and walk off down the road to process. If your man does these things, he's just plain weird. Often—like 95 percent of the time—he's silent as he processes. He's still with you, but he goes quiet as the wheels in his head turn over what you've said, and a response is prepared. At least, you hope a response is being prepared.

You must learn to live with silence if you want to live in peace and intimacy with a man. Don't fire questions at him in an attempt to keep that particular conversation going. Don't keep talking and talking about the issue, hoping he'll finally respond to something you say. Let a few minutes of silence go by. It won't kill you, and it might give the man a chance to process and respond. As the man gets better at this communication skill, he can use the train and be figuring out his reaction as you're talking.

To really connect in conversation, both partners need to learn their individual roles in the train scenario. I have one set of guidelines for women, and one for men.

WOMEN AND THE TRAIN

Ladies, I'll start with you. First, don't chase the train. By this, I mean don't beg and plead with the man in an attempt to hold him in the conversation. "Oh, please talk to me, open up, don't go." This is demeaning for you and turns the man off. It's like grabbing at his pants leg, and it will not open him up. He won't say: "Honey, I feel your pain. You really need me to talk personally now, don't you? I wasn't going to, but I'll do it. I can't stand to see you suffer." Dream on. He'll stiffen up like a board.

In many of the train scenes in my favorite old movies, the man is leaving the woman behind at the station. He's going to war or off on business or on some dangerous mission. They embrace on the platform, he boards the train, and he waves at her from his window seat. Somehow, even though he boards at the last possible second, he gets a window seat right across from where the woman is standing.

As the train slowly, oh so slowly, pulls out of the station, the desperate woman follows the man down the platform. She walks and then runs to keep up with her husband's train car. "No, oh please, no. Don't go. Come back." Pathetic.

Have some dignity. Some poise. Some composure. Let him go on the train without an emotional fuss. Even if he does feel badly for you, which he doesn't, he still can't talk to you without the train trip.

Second, don't try to stop him from getting on the train. This is the aggressive approach. You pull a gun and say: "It's been twelve years, Bob. I'm through waiting. Share now. Start talking or you die. You step on that train, and you're history!"

When you women get through talking to the man, you want an immediate response, don't you? Admit it. You want him to say something personal right after you're done expressing yourself. Well, men can't give you an immediate reaction. We don't want to, that's true. But it's also true that we can't do it.

I love my wife, Sandy. I am a highly verbal, expressive man. I am a clinical psychologist, trained to help others identify and express their deepest feelings and secrets. I teach couples how to communicate in Marriage Enrichment workshops across the country. And guess what? I can't respond immediately in a personal way with Sandy in conversation.

If Sandy tries to force me to talk and aggressively blocks my access to the train, I shut down and give her nothing. Plus, I'm mad at her and want to get away from her. Ladies, if I can't do it, your man can't do it. Let your man get on the train.

Third, don't wait at the station. If you wait, tapping your foot impatiently, it means you have no life. And you are putting more pressure on the man. He can see you back there with the mean, exasperated look on your face. If there's one thing a man can't stand, it's pressure to talk. It drives him insane. It drives him as far away from you as he can get. He could be sitting two feet from you, but emotionally he's two hundred miles away. So when he gets on the train and the train pulls away, leave the station. Get away from there! Do you want to spend the rest of your life waiting for your man to share with you? Go into town and develop a life of your own.

Ladies, it's his job to find you when he returns. Once you've expressed on a subject and asked a few questions, don't bring it up again. Don't stare at him expectantly. Don't give him the look that says: "Well? Say something! My hair is turning gray." Don't give those big, deep sighs of annoyance. Don't pout with your lips pressed together in that tight, rigid line.

Just relax and let some silence go by. Smile. Enjoy the scenery. Close your eyes and imagine yourself on the beach at Waikiki. After a few minutes, if you feel like it, talk about something else. By leaving the station and putting no direct pressure on the man, you just might get him into the pursuit mode. It's like bargaining with a foreign shopkeeper. You make your offer and then walk away. You act as if you don't care about the item in question. What does the shopkeeper do? He doesn't want to lose the deal, so he pursues you and restarts the process. When you're standing with the shopkeeper, even if you're silent, he can tell by your body language and demeanor that you really want the item. So, he won't make any concessions. But when you begin to leave, all of a sudden his confidence evaporates, and he chases you.

I'm not suggesting your husband will break as easily as a Tijuana merchant and scamper after you. Husbands are tougher nuts to crack. But the principle is the same. Cultivate an easy, relaxed silence. Act as if you don't care too awfully much if he responds to what you've said. You are the calm, cool, confident woman whose whole evening won't be ruined if he doesn't respond to you right away.

Remember, he won't talk even if he feels sorry for you. He won't talk just because you want him to. He won't talk, not even a little bit, if he feels pressured by your impatient silence and body language. He'll talk when he's good and ready. He'll talk to a woman he respects. He'll talk to a woman who gives him space and time to process.

MEN AND THE TRAIN

Men, it's your turn. Your job is to learn to use the train in the right way. Do you want real closeness with your woman? Do you want real peace and companionship in the relationship? Do you want to avoid conflict with an angry, resentful woman? Do you want the best sex you've ever had? I know the answer is yes, at least to the last question. All this can be yours if you follow these guidelines.

First, don't board the train without a warning. This isn't fair, and it's downright rude. When you simply shut down in conversation and give the woman zero response, you show her a lack of respect. It's like slapping her across the face. She's left hanging, wondering what's going on in your head. She's hurt. She's frustrated. She thinks all kinds of things about you, none of them flattering.

Now, I know you're not able to give her an immediate response. I've covered that. You've got to think through what she's said, and you've got to use the train to do it. But you can tell her you're getting on the train. You can tell her you need some space to cogitate and meditate before you can regurgitate. (Okay, I got a little carried away with my "tates.")

Men, come up with a phrase you can use to alert the woman your train is leaving. "I'm getting on the train now." "Let me think about that." "I'm going to do some processing, and I'll get back to you." Stating out loud that you're about to board the train is good for the woman, it's good for you, and it keeps the conversation on track. The woman feels respected, knows you heard what she said, and can more comfortably wait for your reply. Mentioning your need to process helps you, the man, actually do it. It's your own verbal signal to start preparing your response. If you don't say it out loud, chances are very good you won't do it.

It's hard to use the train and dig down for a deeper, more personal response. You have to fight your male tendency to sidestep the woman and never respond. Fight this tendency by saying, to the woman and to yourself: "Honey, I'm getting on the train." Now it's out in the open. You've made a deal, and chances are you'll follow through.

Another payoff for telling the woman it's train time is that the conversation is protected and given the opportunity to continue. It's so very easy to derail (don't you just love all these train terms?) a conversation. If—I should say when—the woman reacts negatively to your complete silence, you have murdered the conversation.

Without your train time signal, something bad is bound to happen. It might not. Maybe the woman can maintain her composure and think positive thoughts. But women are sensitive creatures and need to be handled softly and gently. Peter, Jesus' close disciple (and a married man), wrote:

> *You husbands in the same way, live with your wives*
> *in an understanding way, as with someone weaker,*
> *since she is a woman; and show her honor as a fellow*
> *heir of the grace of life, so that your prayers will not be*
> *hindered.*   1 PETER 3:7, NAS

Why gamble with maybe when you can be sure you won't hurt her and kill the conversation?

Your responsibility as the man is to let the woman know when you need to do some processing. This is 1 Peter 3:7 in action. It's a nice, gentle way of telling your wife you've heard enough from her on a particular topic. What you're saying is: "Honey, thanks for sharing. Now, it's my turn to find out my reaction to what you've said." Then the woman can relax and avoid all the potentially nasty reactions I've mentioned. Plus, the conversation is still alive! You can continue it at a later time, when you're back from the train trip. The sun is shining, the grass is growing, and everybody's happy.

The second guideline for the train is: Don't board the train and then never come back. Use the train only to look inside yourself and return to talk. The train is not an escape! It is the method given to you by God to prepare you to talk to your woman.

Almost every married man is a master at escaping a personal talk with his wife. He is a conversational Houdini. He has a variety of tricks in his escape bag. Some are subtle and diabolically clever. Some are harsh and crude. But they all serve the same purpose: to sneak away from the woman at the first whiff of intimacy.

Men, I hate to be the one to tell you this, but here goes. You married her, and now you're going to have to talk to her. And I don't mean talk about a bunch of superficial stuff she could get from a neighbor or the mailman. I mean the deeper stuff buried inside you. Actually, I'm not really the one telling you to open up. God is. Read Ephesians 5:25, and then try to convince me it's God's will for you to cut the woman off from your personal, inside life. The fact is, you can only love your wife as Christ loved the church by letting her inside.

God, being gracious, has provided the train as one of the main ways for you to express personally with your wife. He intends you to buy a round-trip ticket for your train rides. You're coming back to talk! Christ doesn't leave the church hanging, so don't leave your wife hanging.

I was speaking one weekend in Chicago and had just described my train example when a man raised his hand. He said: "You're talking about a loop train." I told him he was absolutely right. Loop trains, often found in large cities like

Chicago, form one large circle around the city. No matter where you board the train, if you stay on long enough, it will come back to your starting point.

Finally, men, don't expect the woman to come back to the train station and initiate. It's not her job to restart the conversation after your train trip. It's your job! If she initiates, the same old control-closeness problem will rear its incredibly ugly head. She'll be the crowbar, and so, automatically, you'll be the clam. Another conversation will bite the dust.

You find her, wherever she is, and start talking. If it was a short train trip, it will be easy to find her. She'll be sitting in the car next to you, at a table in the restaurant, or beside you on the couch in your home. If the train trip took longer, several hours or one day or more, you'll have to go out of your way to find her. She could be in the yard, at her job, or in bed reading. However long your train trip and wherever she is when you're back, go to her and share what you've found.

The pad idea I described in Chapter Five will also serve you well in the train process. Guys, if the woman has talked about an important subject and it'll take you a while to process, use the pad. In the presence of the woman, jot down the following: the subject, any questions she wants you to answer about the subject, and what she specifically wants you to comment on in your response.

Recently, Sandy and I had a big discussion on the education of our kids. Actually, she had most of the discussion. She buried me in emotions, facts, impressions, rabbit trails, and questions. I needed the train badly. I told her I'd get back to her. Then, immediately, I jotted down on my pad:

Subject: our children's education

Sandy's questions:

1. Should we homeschool, keep the kids in private Christian school, or send them to public school?

2. What's best for the kids and our family?

3. What can we afford?

Sandy wants to know:

1. How I feel about these options, pros and cons. What I think God wants us to do.

I put all this down on my pad right in front of her. That seemed to impress her, and she agreed to wait for my response. I used my pad notes to think, pray, and process the next day and a half. As I came up with responses and feelings, what did I do with them? Did I just file them away in my male brain and hope I could retrieve them when I talked to Sandy? Are you kidding? I put down on my pad what I found on my train trip! That way, I was prepared to face Sandy and her memory with confidence. Then, I took my pad, and I went to her and began sharing my views on the education of our children.

If there's one thing I've learned in sixteen years of marriage, it's to come back to Sandy on a subject and be prepared. If I don't have my ducks in a row, it's not pretty. In fact, it's humiliating. Sandy will remember, without a pad, every single point of the previous discussion. She will recall, with her devastatingly accurate memory, everything she wanted to know from me.

Some of you men are laughing at this pad idea. Don't

laugh. You follow this kind of write-it-down, organized approach in your business life, don't you? I'll bet you'd jot down some particulars if you had to get back to your boss or an important client, wouldn't you? How much more important is your dear, precious wife than persons you interact with on your job? You know the answer.

You'll forget to get back to your wife if you don't use the pad. You might feel stupid jotting down a topic on which you need to respond to your wife. But you'll feel a whole lot more stupid when you forget and have nothing to say to her. Real men, real godly men, use the pad. And use the pad to remind you to tell her how your train trip, your processing, is going. She needs to be given updates on your progress to keep her from reacting negatively and to keep the conversation alive.

Please understand it's difficult for the woman to wait for your response, especially if it's taking you more than several hours. She needs to know how you're doing. She needs some hope. For example, I might jot down on my pad: "Tell Sandy I'm still working on the whole school situation. I'll be ready to talk tonight." Then, I call her and give her the message. That's a loving, understanding husband. That's an Ephesians 5:25 and 1 Peter 3:7 husband.

You can also use your trusty pad to jot down things going on in your wife's life. These are items she's interested in, personally involved in, or concerned about in her daily life. It might be a problem at her work, a difficult situation with a child, or a positive, fun activity she's pursuing. These are subjects on which she has not asked you to comment. She may or may not have brought them up in conversation. But you're smart enough to know (at least, you are now) she'd love you to bring these subjects up in conversation.

Case in point. One day I was home for lunch and spent about twenty minutes talking with Sandy. It was a little choppy because three-year-old William was banging around the table. Anyway, I became aware of three areas of interest in Sandy's life during that lunch. Two she mentioned in our conversation. One I overheard on a phone call she had with a friend at the end of our time together. Before I left for work, I took my "home" pad down from the hutch and made these notes:

Ask Sandy tonight in our talk time about:

1. Her computer game against Trish

2. Her vest craft project

3. Her progress on the talent show slide presentation

She didn't ask me what I thought or felt about these three things. She didn't ask me to ride the train and then talk to her that night about them. Now, if she had, I would have used the pad, taken the train, used the pad again to put down my responses, and then talked to her that night.

But this was my own idea. When I brought out my pad that night and asked her about these areas, I scored some serious love points. Or something like that. She really felt like I loved her, cared about her, and cherished her as a person. And all because of my little pad.

Men, you can use the pad to jot down a note saying you couldn't find anything inside during the train trip. This happens. You rode the train, maybe even a couple of times, but came up empty. If that's the case, then tell her that. She'll ask why nothing came up. Women always ask why. Just do your best to explain why you think nothing came up. You may have no idea. If you recognize what's blocking you from that particular subject, tell her.

If you don't want to talk about a subject, jot down a note stating that and let the woman know. Include the reasons and when, if ever, you'll be ready to ride the train and give her a reaction to this sensitive topic. One of the pad's great relationship benefits is that it gives the woman closure. She needs to close the conversational door on subjects she has brought up to you. There is nothing worse—just about—than a woman without closure.

Jot down what she wants to know. Ride the train. Whatever your response is, jot it down on the pad and tell her. Emotionally, she can move on when you have responded. You have completed your end of the conversation. You see, a real conversation isn't over until you've given your response to what the woman has said. Without your response, the exchange is incomplete. It's cookies without milk. It's Mutt without Jeff. It's waffles without syrup. It's like a catcher catching a fastball from his pitcher and holding the ball. He refuses to throw it back. The game is stopped. It's over until the catcher throws the ball back.

When you give no response to the woman, the conversation is over. There is no connection. There is no interaction. There is no intimacy. There is one upset woman, and one dead conversation.

Even when you give a response, the conversation's not over. Hopefully, it's just the beginning. You've completed one cycle, and that's good. What's better is to continue and complete a number of cycles. The more cycles of comment and response you create, the deeper the two of you will get.

The best conversations last awhile. God created men and women to engage in long, stimulating conversations that produce the best kind of intimacy on earth. Let me show you how to make a real conversation.

ELEVEN

A GREAT TALK TAKES TIME

In America, we demand instant gratification. Everything has to be fast. I mean, everything. We want what we want now. Right now. Speed is critical to life. Don't make me wait, or somebody's going to get hurt.

We get up in the morning, clap the light on, and take a quick shower. After a brief blow-dry of the hair and a couple of snappy strokes with the speed stick deodorant, we hit the kitchen running. We wolf down one bowl of instant oatmeal or drink a powdered breakfast mix. Then, we gulp the brew produced by the faithful and fast coffeemaker on our way to the car. With the touch of a button, we open the garage door. Another button opens the car door, and after we climb in, a button locks all the doors. Whirring, the seat belt slides around us, and off we go. We could move from zero to sixty in twenty seconds if we only had the deserted, open road enjoyed by the drivers in the television commercials.

As we commute we can use the cell phone to make a few quick calls and, luckily, don't have to worry that no one can reach us while we're talking. Call waiting will help, and if that jams up, the beeper will save us. When we finally get to the office, everything there is as fast as we can stand it. We've got the phone lines, fax machine, and a wonderful computer system (when it works). We've got E-mail, Internet access, eight hundred thousand super-mega-giga bytes of memory, and a laser printer that flies over the page. The computer is upgraded every two weeks because somebody, somewhere, keeps making a faster chip.

Lunch is—what else—fast food. Zipping along the drive-thru lane, we make a few cell calls and spend a few minutes on our incredibly small and unbelievably fast laptop.

When we get back home, the microwave zaps our frozen dinner. Cups and plates and silverware go in the dishwasher, and the rest of the evening just keeps getting quicker. Pop in a video for the kids, and it's instant entertainment. With the television remote control in hand, we can clip through one hundred cable channels if we feel like it and get instant news as it breaks around the globe. Or we can use our home computer to play scores of games, talk to people thousands of miles away in real time, or rapidly surf the Net. All the knowledge of the universe is just a few keystrokes away.

Life is good because life is fast. Waiting is a dirty word. We refuse to wait. We can't stand to wait! I want it now! Didn't you hear me? If our fast world slows down, we simmer and boil, and our blood pressure skyrockets. We have a hissy fit if there are three persons ahead of us in the supermarket express checkout line. Oh no, that lady has a whole stack of coupons! This could take an extra five minutes!

It's an outrage if we hit two red lights in a row. It's got to be a conspiracy of traffic engineers to slow us down. There's no excuse—none—for the lady with the big hair to be going the speed limit in front of us. Everybody, except her, knows you can go five miles over the limit and not get pulled over by the police. Isn't that in the Constitution?

We die a slow, hideous death in the driver's license bureau. It's a nightmare to rot on a metal folding chair and wait for our number, one hundred eighty-eight, to be called. All we can do is stare at the amazingly relaxed employees moving in slow motion. To add insult to injury, at the end of the process we walk away with the worst picture ever taken of us. We're either grinning like a fool or looking like we've just been booked on a first-degree murder charge.

All this emphasis on speed transfers to our relationships. We tend to think we should get instant love, too. I mean, why not? Except for a driver's license, we can get everything else fast. Intimacy ought to be quick, right? Wrong.

God has designed men and women to develop closeness slowly, with considerable effort and over time. We can get instant oatmeal. We cannot get instant intimacy. Intimacy with a member of the opposite sex requires, absolutely requires, connection in conversation. And connecting in conversation doesn't ever happen quickly.

Great marriages are a series of great conversations. Every good and intimate experience in marriage comes out of a great talk. Compromise. Conflict resolution. Exposing who you really are. Passionate sex. They all flow out of great talks. And a great talk takes time—measured not in minutes, but in hours and days. It takes time to move together through the layers of resistance, and chitchat, and gender differences, down to the good stuff. We have to keep a conversation going and prevent it from dying prematurely in order to reach the gold.

Many couples barely touch on conversational topics and drop them before they can develop into a deeper connection. If there's not an immediate spark, forget it. If one partner isn't interested in the subject right away, it's dumped in the ditch, and we move on. If we hang up on one of our male-female communication differences, it's easier just to bail out of the talk.

All great conversations happen in stages. That's why the train works! They start out very small—insignificant really —and slowly grow into something beautiful and stimulating. It's like a long, exciting tennis rally. Actually, it's more like a challenging tennis match between two very different players. There are ups and downs. Pauses. Unpredictable turns. Flashes of insight. Bursts of energy. But in this conversational tennis match, both partners can win. That's what God wants. The partners have to follow some simple and effective rules. The partners must keep doing their individual parts to keep the rallies, and the match, going.

How to Make a Great Conversation

Here's the deal the two of you make. The woman allows the man his time and space to process. She realizes his need for the train and lets him board without resistance. The man agrees to find out what's inside, come back to the woman, and initiate the talk.

Here's how it works. You will have a series of talks on the same topic. Deep, complete sharing happens in stages. Always, always, always. No couple reaches deep, complete sharing on one topic in one sitting. That's impossible. (Anyone who says it can be done is delusional, a liar, or just doesn't get it.) It's not deep sharing right away because the man and the woman have to work together to get there. The man certainly isn't ready right away. Frankly, neither is the woman.

God's master plan for opposite sex conversation is that step-by-step we get deeper and deeper as we feed off each other's feelings and reactions and insights.

Let's take a look at the stages of a great conversation. First, a review of how to use the train.

Ladies, before he boards the train, when you're talking together, it's okay for you to share as completely as you can. The woman usually starts the conversational ball rolling in this introductory stage. That's fine. There's nothing wrong with that. Ladies, feel free to ask questions and raise issues you want him to comment on when he's ready. *When he's ready* is the key phrase. Don't be controlling and don't expect deeper expression from him at this time.

Men, jot down on your pad the subject and what the woman wants to know. Then, jump on the train and process. Come back and give the woman your response. Share a few comments, maybe even a feeling or two. Tell her what you've found out so far.

Next: The woman hears the man out and reacts to what he shares. What he says triggers some more thoughts and feelings in her. She spontaneously tells him what has come up inside her. Then he takes in her response and gets back on the train to do some more processing. He comes back again and shares his new response, getting a little more personal this time. The woman listens and responds to what he says. He rides the train again, comes back and shares, and she responds again.

I think you get the idea. It might be four, five, or six separate talks on the same topic before the man really gets deep and expresses what's inside. The whole process may take two hours or four days. It all depends on the particular topic, the personalities of the partners, and what level of intimacy is desired.

This is teamwork. It is working together to achieve a deep conversation. The longer you dialogue on a topic, the deeper and closer you're going to get. Each time the man returns from the train, he gets a little deeper, and the woman gets a little deeper. We respond to each other! Cycles of comment and response, sandwiched around the man's train trips, create connection and intimacy.

"Boy, when you said that, it made me think and feel this! When I said that, it jogged your memory of that great time at the beach two summers ago. Hearing you talk about the beach made me think about. . ."

Some of the best talks Sandy and I have happen over two or three days, sometimes four or five days, as we revisit issues. We touch on all angles of an issue. We get in touch with our emotions. We get beneath the surface to the good stuff. To the "why we got married" stuff.

The train helps you work together to talk through issues and avoid letting them die unresolved. You need to keep bringing up the same topics until you've squeezed out of them every last drop of depth and intimacy.

I have some good news for you, men. Even though the train trips will always be necessary, they get shorter with practice. You can get pretty fast at processing. Not as fast as a woman, but pretty fast. Granted, when you're learning the train skill, it will be difficult and tedious. But like any other skill, if you practice, you will improve. It will become second nature and will even get to be fun.

Our old friends, Bob and Betty, want to show you how to use the train and build a conversation in stages. First, they will demonstrate a regular, positive talk. Second, they'll illustrate the way to work through a conflict over time.

Two Days to Intimacy

Bob and Betty are in the family room. They've put the kids to bed and are just settling in for their daily thirty-minute talk. They learned the importance of this once-a-day conversation time at one of Dr. David Clarke's Marriage Enrichment weekends.

> Betty: "You wouldn't believe the phone call I had with my mother today!" (Betty is upset because Mom criticized her handling of a situation with the kids.) "Mom lectured me and put her usual guilt trip on me. It made me cry, and it made me mad. I'm tired of her putting me down." Betty proceeds to give the blow-by-blow, she said-I said account of the talk with her mother.

> Bob: "Sorry, honey. What a rotten call. Bummer." He doesn't have too much to say. He makes a few general comments and sympathy noises.

> Betty: Bob's response is not what she really needs,

and she tells him so. "Bob, when you're ready, I want a little feedback on this mother thing. Am I overreacting? Am I too hard on the kids, like she says? What do you feel about my relationship with my mother?"

Bob: "I'll get back to you. My mind's a blank." He jots down some notes on his pad. They move on to another topic.

Later that night, just before bed:

Bob: "You know, I was thinking about that call. It makes me mad. She shouldn't have treated you that way. You're a great mom. I'll bet you're tired of never quite pleasing the woman. That one comment she made about your temper. . .what a crock! She had no right."

Betty: "Thanks, honey. I appreciate you saying that. It helps. I do feel like I never please her. Back in second grade, I did a science fair project. As I was leaving the house with it, she said: 'Well, I hope you get a passing grade on that thing.' I cried all the way to school."

The next morning at breakfast. They have a few minutes together before the kids arrive at the table:

Bob: "How many times did your mom say I love you and give you positive reinforcement? Where was your dad in all this? I feel badly for you.

Your self-esteem has really taken some hits."

Betty is delighted he's pursuing the issue. She loves it when he asks her questions. She easily answers his questions and talks freely about her childhood. She also brings up current examples of her lack of self-esteem. She feels close to Bob. She feels as though he cares about her.

Later that evening:

Bob: "Talking about that phone call with your mom made me think about me and my dad. He was sure hard to please. He was gruff and didn't give many compliments. One day, after a Little League baseball game, he chewed me out in front of the group over. . ."

Betty: "I can't believe he did that! One time my mom came into my room on prom night and. . ."

Bob and Betty talk about their childhoods and how they were treated by their parents. They comfort each other and feel closer. They can identify, and even feel, each other's pain. They resolve to help each other in the area of self-esteem and to treat their own kids differently.

Can you see the progression of intimacy? It may seem too good to be true, but it's not. This could happen on a regular basis for you and your spouse. You just have to stay with a conversation and go through the stages.

With some practice, you'll learn how to have three or four separate conversations going at once during the week. Now, they all won't pan out. You'll get different levels of intimacy and depth. Sometimes, a conversation trails off and ends up a dud. Sometimes, you do pretty well and get a reasonably decent level of closeness. Not earthshaking, but nice. Sometimes, you strike gold and get very deep. When you're working on simultaneous multiple conversations, your chances of hitting a winner go way up.

Four Days to Finish a Fair Fight

You're thinking: "Four days for a fight? You've got to be kidding." No, I'm not kidding. It can easily take four days to work through a conflict and reach some kind of resolution. If it's a big issue, it can take longer.

Anger and hurt are nasty, powerful emotions. You've got to give yourselves time to express and sort through them. The best way to do this is in stages. You keep chipping away at a conflict until all the feelings are released, the two points of view are expressed and understood, and a plan of action is in place.

The Bible teaches that anger needs to be expressed and released on the first day of a conflict. Ephesians 4:26 states: "Be angry, and yet do not sin; do not let the sun go down on your anger" (NAS). But that doesn't mean the conflict is over. Oh, no! There are other steps that must be taken, and several more days will be required to complete the process.

As you might imagine, men and women have very different communication styles during a conflict. This is a major reason why conflicts are so painful and take time to get through.

THE HIGH-TECH
FOOD PROCESSOR
AND THE KITCHEN WORKER

The woman is the High-Tech Food Processor in a conflict. When a woman is angry and hurt, she speeds up and starts spewing out a torrent of words. She slices and dices at warp speed, churning out a huge mound of emotional debris.

The man in a conflict is a ninety-five-year-old Kitchen Worker with arthritis in his hands and a dull knife. When conflict breaks out, a man slows way down. He needs time and space to sort the vegetables and cut them into pieces. He works at a slow and uneven pace, pausing often to rest and make sure he's doing a quality job.

The High-Tech Food Processor and the elderly Kitchen Worker are side by side at the counter. Their job is to work together to process a large pile of vegetables. What happens when the food processor is on high power and the top blows off? Pandemonium breaks out! All the chopped-up food erupts and sprays the room in a wild, unpredictable rush. What does the old man do when he's in danger of being killed by thousands of flying vegetable bits? He leaves the room. He flees to safety! Can you blame him?

The man feels out of control in a conflict. He is often over-whelmed by the emotional intensity of the woman. Ladies, give him time to think and process. He needs the train more than ever when a conflict surfaces. And, ladies, please keep your food processor on—at most—medium power. And keep the lid on. He'll still have to leave the kitchen a number of times, but at least he won't be soaked in your vegetable spray.

Now, to Bob and Betty and their conflict. It's a weekday morning. Betty is marching down the hall with that "look" on her face. Bob isn't fast enough and gets trapped on the recliner. Betty says those four words that Bob hates to hear: "We need to talk." She might as well say: "It's time to suffer. Would you like me to use the rawhide whip or the buzz saw?"

Betty: "I'm angry because you didn't help Johnny get his clothes on. I asked you to do it, you said yes, but it didn't happen. So, I had to do it." Betty gives a detailed description of how Johnny fought her tooth and nail as she dressed him. "Then I saw the hole in his bedroom wall. Well, that did it. I asked you to patch that hole three months ago! Bob, this house is falling down around us and you don't seem to care!"

Bob: "Betty, look, this is not a good time." He's defensive, quiet, a little huffy.

Betty: Thinks to herself: *There's never a good time.* But, she doesn't say it.

Bob: "I've got to leave for work. Let's meet tonight and discuss it." In his car, he puts the conflict issue down on his pad.

Lunchtime:

Bob: He calls Betty on the phone and says: "Honey, I've been thinking about this morning. I want to get things back to an even keel between us. I have something to say tonight."

Betty: Thinks to herself: *Don't tease me. Don't make me wait. Tell me now. At least give me a hint.* But she's learned that being patient works better than snide comments, so she replies, "Good. See you tonight. Thanks for calling."

That evening:

Bob: Consults his pad and says: "I'm sorry you had to dress Johnny this morning. I just forgot. I was going to do it, but it slipped my mind. I'll try to do better."

Betty: "Thanks for the apology, Bob. It's a bigger issue than just Johnny's clothes this morning, though. I feel overworked, overstressed, and underappreciated. Why, in the last six months, I've. . ." She recites a litany of all the jobs she's done and shares how exhausted she's been.

Bob: "It's been this bad for six months?" He's stunned, blown away. "I thought we were doing just fine. Man, I don't know what to tell you. I'm pulling my weight around here, aren't I? I'm doing more than a lot of guys I know." He stops and stares off into space.

Betty: "I want you to think about the jobs you do around here. Then, think about what I do. I just want your honest assessment."

Bob: "Okay. I'll do it. Let me ride the train. I'll get back to you."

Day Two is a busy one. The kids had some ball games, homework went a little long, and everything ran overtime.

The whole family watched a movie together, and then the kids went to bed. Bob and Betty have a brief talk time just before bed:

> Betty: When it looks pretty certain Bob's not going to bring up the conflict issue, she reminds him. "Bob, remember you agreed to think about the jobs we each do around the house? When you're ready, I'd like to talk about that. Okay?"

> Bob: "Oh yeah, Betty. Sorry. I didn't use my pad, and I totally forgot. I'm writing it down now." They talk about a few other topics and feel connected, even though their on-going conflict is not yet resolved.

The third day, at evening talk time:

> Bob: "Honey, I can see that the balance of labor is way out of whack. I started thinking of all the jobs you do around here and couldn't count them all. I didn't have any trouble listing the jobs I do. I can see why you're so tired and irritable all the time. I've come up with a list of extra jobs I want to do on a regular basis."

> Betty: "I'm glad you can understand what I've been going through." They work on the list together and finalize the specifics of Bob's new jobs. They talk about it when Bob gets home, and this prompts Betty to say: "You know, Bob. I'd like to talk about your work schedule. It seems like you're getting home later and later all the

time. Plus, it's unpredictable, and I can't plan dinner too well."

Bob: He's a little defensive and annoyed. He hears a high-tech food processor warming up. "Honey, I'm about talked out on this subject for tonight. Let's deal with that tomorrow."

Betty reluctantly agrees to shut it down.

The fourth day, at evening talk time:

Bob: "I was frustrated last night when you brought up the issue of when I get home. I thought about it, and I guess it is a little unpredictable. Things come up, and I have to deal with them. What can I do to help you?"

Betty: "I need to have a rough idea of when you'll be home. Can you call me at five o'clock and give me, within thirty minutes, a time frame?"

Bob: "Yeah, let's try that. Believe me, sweetheart, I want to be home with you and the kids." He puts down on his pad a note to remind him of the deal: "Put in planner every day at 5 P.M. to call Betty about when I'll be home."

Again, can you see the progressive nature of this conflict conversation? I'm convinced that, with both regular and conflict-resolving conversations, God's design is for couples to talk in stages over several days. Conflict talks naturally take longer because they are difficult and intense. If you try to speed them up, you'll make a big mess. An already painful situation will become a disaster. Not only do you not reach a solution, you both end up resentful and farther apart.

Work together towards talking in stages. Use the train. I'm telling you, it will make a tremendous difference in your communication. You'll get more emotional connections. You'll resolve more conflicts. You'll be a little closer every day.

TWELVE

TRAIN TRIPS
THAT NEVER END

I know what you ladies are thinking. You're thinking: Dave, I like what you're saying about the train. Building a conversation with my husband in stages sounds great. I know I have to be patient and give him time to process. Believe me, I can handle my end of the program because I'll do anything to have intimate conversations with my husband.

But, you're thinking, *there's one major flaw in this cleverly designed system. You are assuming the man will ride the train and come back to talk. Who do you think you're kidding? What*

*do I do if my husband does not return from a train trip?
Actually, I shouldn't say* if. *I should say* when *he doesn't return.*

Ladies, I don't blame you for thinking this way. You've lived with a man long enough to know the sad realities of marital communication. You've been burned thousands of times. You've been left holding the conversational bag with no man in sight. He may never have returned from a train trip. You have a right to be skeptical.

WHAT IF
HE NEVER COMES BACK?

I'm here to help. That's my job. When the man doesn't come back from the train and talk to you, there are two actions you can take.

First, go out and buy a little electric train set. A locomotive, several cars, a caboose, and the track. Set it up in a corner of your home. When your husband does not come back to talk to you, plug the train set in and run it. The train will steam around the circle and make that distinctive train sound: *chugga-chugga, chugga-chugga.* The locomotive will blow its whistle loud and clear: *woo-woo, woo-woo.* Your husband will hear the train and realize he's not returned from a train trip. It'll be your indirect signal for him to come back and restart the conversation. You don't have to say a word.

Second, you can buy a stack of professionally made cards with a picture of a train on them. Keep these in your purse and in a handy place in your home. When it looks like he's not coming back to talk, simply walk up and hand him a train card. The card will jog his memory about the subject you two were discussing.

Of course, I'm joking with these two ideas. You don't want to humiliate or embarrass your husband. It may be tempting at times, but I don't recommend it. As Gene Kelly said so eloquently in *Singing in the Rain* when describing his career and relationships: "Dignity. . . always dignity."

Seriously, here's what you can do when your husband shows no sign of returning to you to talk about an issue. You are allowed one—that's one—low-key reminder. In a reasonable, normal, nonsarcastic tone, you say to him: "Honey, have you thought about that issue we discussed? When you're ready, I'd like to talk about it." That's it. No brow-beating. No whining. No begging. No yelling. No guilt trips. If you bring it up any more than once, you are a nag. And, you're creating more resistance, not less. He'll feel pressured, controlled, and you'll hear the unpleasant sound of a clam slamming shut.

Tell your husband that you will remind him only one time to return to talk to you. This is just a one-time informational statement to the man. Just tell him: "Bob, I want to talk about our communication and my tendency to nag you to respond to issues we've discussed. From now on, I will only remind you once about a topic I want to continue talking about." In this same informational conversation, ask him how he wants you to remind him. If he doesn't like the two-sentence prompt I have suggested, fine. Ask him exactly what words he wants you to use. You'll do it just the way he wants. That way he'll feel more in control.

When to prompt: A good rule of thumb is the bigger and more important the issue, the longer you should wait before reminding him. It will take him longer to process a bigger issue. You may wait two to four days and then remind. For less critical issues, you don't have to wait as long.

Anywhere from thirty minutes to eight hours is reasonable. Certainly, by the end of the day this less critical issue can be brought up.

Also, it's a good idea to use your one reminder when you have the man's undivided attention. Like, during your daily conversation time in the evenings, for example. With no distractions and already being in a conversational mode, the man is more likely to hear the reminder and respond to it.

Even though my suggestions about the toy train and cards were meant in jest, there may be a germ of practical truth in them. Some men prefer to be reminded to restart a talk in indirect, nonverbal ways. These men cringe at the thought of the woman verbally reminding them. No matter how nicely she does it, they hate it and clam up. If your man is in this category of nonverbal prompts, no problem. Ask him what he wants you to do.

One couple I worked with used their own technique. When the wife wanted her husband to talk about an issue they had discussed earlier, she would fill a cup with tea and place it on his bedside table. He'd see the full cup and know she wanted to continue to the next stage of a conversation. For him, it was a gentle, nonthreatening signal. Hey, whatever works!

You could have some fun with this. Encourage him to come up with some zany, creative way for you to remind him. Some men respond better when humor is used. (They can't feel controlled when they're laughing.) Hang panty hose on the ceiling fan. Hide the television remote control. Give him a paper plate for dinner instead of a regular one. Play a funny, romantic song he has preselected on the CD player. Send him an E-mail message. Write him a note. Hand him a candy bar or some other favorite treat with a

note attached: "Talk to your wife, and I'm yours to enjoy."
The bottom line is, do the prompting any way he wants.

HE WON'T RESPOND EVERY TIME

Ladies, I'm sure this won't come as a complete shock to you,
but here's a brutal fact you need to know. Even if you use my
brilliant communication techniques, the man won't come back
and talk to you on every issue. (That would be communication heaven, and life down here on earth just isn't that good.)
You can't expect him to respond to every single thing you say.
You say too much! There aren't enough hours in the day for
him to process and get back to you on all the topics you
bring up. He simply can't keep up with the kind of volume
you produce. He's like the poor assembly-line worker who
falls behind and can't quite catch up.

You need to have realistic expectations. At first, he'll be
very close to where he is now: zero return train trips. Don't get
discouraged. After several months of the two of you practic-
ing communication in stages, his percentage will start to rise.
If he learns to use the train and comes back to talk 30 to 50
percent of the time, that's good! In fact, that's great! That percentage is more than enough to build great conversations that
will make your marriage all that God intended.

I have worked very hard on my train trips the last few
years. In my best week, I only return to Sandy to continue
50 percent of our conversations. This is my own idea, and I
can't get any higher than 50 percent! And that's even after
she gives me a reminder.

The good news is: You don't have to be anywhere near 100
percent to build an intimate relationship. Sandy and I have

found that if I can hit a return rate of 30 to 50 percent in a week, that's enough. We will complete these conversations and usually get deeply connected on one or two of them.

In a typical week, Sandy and I will start at least thirty conversations. Most of these peter out quickly and die a quick and natural death. We end up working on maybe eight conversations. If I return to talk to Sandy on four of these conversations, then our chances of connecting on a deeper level are excellent. If we hit the big-time on just one of these completed talks, that's good enough.

That's right. We have discovered that just one intimate conversation a week keeps us emotionally, physically, and spiritually close. The whole week is energized by this one talk that clicked. Some weeks we get more than one winner of a talk. When that happens, it's really tremendous. Frankly, it's rare that we get more than one. We have busy lives, daily hassles, and four kids. One is enough for us. One will be enough for you.

Rate Your Conversations

Ladies, I think you realize by now that you can't get away with prompting the man to respond to every topic. That's nagging, pure and simple. You will drive him crazy and kill your chances of conversational closeness.

Here's a little trick (I should say, technique) that you can use to help your husband respond that 30 to 50 percent of the time: During an introductory conversation, when you are expressing yourself on a topic, tell the man how important it is to you that he get back to you. Rate the conversation on a scale of one to ten, one being next to meaningless, and ten being extremely important to you.

Typically, you'll rate only conversations that are important to you and for which you want a response. When you're
throwing out a lot of conversational tidbits—superficial stuff
—let him decide to respond or not. You don't have to say:
"That's a one, that's a three. . ." If you don't verbally rate
it, he can assume it's not terribly crucial to you. (He'll only
respond if the topic triggers some interest in him.) When
a topic is critical and you really want a response, verbally
give him a high rating: "Bob, this is a nine for me. I need
a response." Anything from a seven to a ten needs to be rated.

The basic guy can't read a woman and figure out on his
own how important a topic is to her. The woman thinks it's
obvious when she desperately wants or needs a response. She
thinks she's giving off incredibly clear signals, and that only an
idiot or a completely uncaring person could miss her message.

Too bad you didn't marry a woman, ladies. She'd pick up
your signals. Your husband isn't an idiot, and he's not uncaring.
He's a man and can only pick up a signal when it hits him
upside the head. So, give him a rating number when it's especially important that he get back to you on a topic. This will
be a clear signal to him, and the odds go up that he'll respond.
If he doesn't respond, restate the rating number when you
prompt him.

If he doesn't respond to your prompt, drop it. If it's a
sensitive and absolutely vital issue, go to him and clean your
system with the one-way communication technique I discussed in Chapter Eight. Then, if a decision simply has to
be made, go ahead and make it without him.

MEN MUST REVISIT

Men, revisiting conversations will be extremely difficult for you to do. Going back to pick up where your wife left off and sharing your reaction isn't natural. It feels strange. It is the exact opposite of how you normally operate in the arena of communication.

You try not to live in the past. You constantly look ahead to the future: to tonight, to tomorrow, to next week, to next year. You hate to rehash old news. You don't want to talk about yesterday or even today. That's over with. Who cares?

Unfortunately, your wife cares. She wants to talk about the past. She's always bringing up issues and events that are over and done with. You don't want to be dragged back to this old stuff. You get annoyed and look for ways to get out of these retroconversations. For you, when a conversation is over, it's over. If she brings up an old issue, you tense up immediately and think: *We already talked about that. Stop beating a dead horse!*

Men, listen to me. To her, the horse isn't dead. It's hardly even born yet! If you stick to your current style of one conversation per topic, you'll never have a great conversation with your wife. That's right! Never! You won't ever be close, really close, to your wife unless you revisit issues and continue conversations. You'll keep looking ahead day after day, month after month, year after year, until. . .you're dead.

I'm not saying you'll be miserable with your wife if you don't learn to build conversations in stages. That's not true. You'll have an okay relationship. It'll be fair. Pretty good. You won't have a whole lot of passion, and sex will be just routine, but that's all right. I mean, sex isn't the most important thing in the world, anyway.

Hey, I didn't get married for this kind of ho-hum, luke-warm relationship. No way! I want the best, the deepest, and the most passionate marriage I can possibly have with Sandy. And you know that's what you want with your wife. To achieve this, you need to revisit conversations.

I know you can handle this revisiting skill because you do it all the time. Think about it. You rehash sporting events with the guys on a regular basis. You talk, in detail and with great emotion, about that last touchdown drive, the winning twenty-five-foot birdie putt, the home run in the ninth inning, and the knockout punch in the tenth round.

In business, you are forced to rehash and rehash and rehash old issues with coworkers and customers. You talk and talk and retalk until you reach a compromise. Until you reach a contract. Until you work out a solution to a problem.

You can do the same thing with your wife. You won't regret it. It'll be a lot more fun than talking sports with the guys and hashing through an issue at work, trust me. Start doing it, and you'll see that I'm right. Give it a two-month trial and see what happens.

WOMEN MUST BE PATIENT

The only thing more difficult than a man forcing himself to revisit a conversation is a woman forcing herself to wait for him to do it. Ladies, it'll just about kill you to hold your tongue while he rides the train and does his processing. It will seem to you that he is moving at the speed of a glacier. You'll be convinced he is deliberately stalling. No one could take that long to think about an issue before he comes back to talk!

Actually, it does take a man that long. There are very few men in the world who can process as quickly as a woman. I doubt very seriously you are married to one of them. The men I meet who can process rapidly are married to women who process very slowly. One way or the other, there's almost always one slow processor in a relationship.

Ladies, you have a doctorate in emotional expression. You're very good at it. In fact, you're world-class. Your husband has struggled only through fifth grade in this field. (I'm being generous.) Give him a break!

I hope I've convinced you that his slower processor is part of God's design for marital communication. Don't see it as some kind of genetic mistake. Don't see it as his way to annoy and frustrate you. Above all, don't try to speed him up. That's right. One of the major mistakes women make in conversation is attempting to "help" the man process information at a higher speed. You just can't stand to wait, can you? You jump into the lull and try to flag down the train, drag the man out, and get him to talk.

Faced with this kind of pressure, well-meaning or not, a man does just one thing. Nothing. Absolutely nothing. Any attempt to artificially speed him up is a serious violation and kills the conversation instantly. Your conversation is road-kill, and you're the one that ran over it, speeding.

Patience is a virtue. It's an especially important virtue when dealing with a man in conversation. Ladies, you need to work hard at developing patience. Practice building up your endurance. A conversation with a man is not a sprint. It's at least a ten-kilometer run. Of course, to you it will feel like an agonizing marathon.

When he's on the train, learn to bite your tongue. Bite the bullet. Bite whatever you have to in order to keep your mouth closed and keep from rushing him. Give him a chance to come back. If he returns to talk on his own, then you've got a conversation that just might go somewhere.

THIRTEEN

BEFORE YOU BOARD THE TRAIN

I know I've provided a valuable public service by explaining the use of the train in a couple's life. It is, I believe, one of the secrets to creating great conversations with the opposite sex.

Men, I've given you a wonderful gift with the train! I know you will appreciate it. There's one little catch, though. There's always a catch, isn't there? I've only given you half the story of the train. There's something very important you must do before you get on the train. It's not an option. It's not window dressing. It's something you just have to get done if you want the train to help you and your wife communicate.

The Negligee or
the Flannel Nightgown?

If you do this "thing," your use of the train can be very successful. You'll be able to focus clearly on finding your personal stuff on the train. There will be no pressure from the woman. You can relax and take your time preparing your response. And when you return, your woman will be ready and eager to hear what you have to say. You'll get a very warm, fuzzy reception.

Here's the picture. You return from the train trip and open the door to your home. You look into the den and feel the heat from the roaring fire in the fireplace. Candles are lit, and music is playing softly. Your wife is curled up in front of the fire, wearing your favorite, skimpy negligee. She turns to you and smiles a warm invitation.

Okay, maybe it isn't that good. But it's close. You do this "thing," and your wife will be pleasant and receptive. And who knows? Maybe the negligee will come later, after your great conversation.

But if you fail to do this thing, just the opposite happens. The train trip will be a waste of time. Chances are, it'll just be an escape. There will be pressure and bad feelings from the woman, so you won't be able to concentrate on your personal stuff, anyway. Even if you do return and want to talk, the woman won't want to hear what you have to say. She could care less. She'll be angry, hurt, and resentful. You'll get an incredibly chilly reception.

Here's the picture. And it's not pretty. When you return

and open the door, your wife is standing in the kitchen. Her arms are crossed, and her hair is in rollers. She is wearing a huge, pup tent of a flannel nightgown that covers her from the neck to the floor. All you can see is her face. But that's enough—she has that look on her face. That look that says: "Touch me and you die. You are a piece of dirty lint on the screen of my life." She will make you suffer. It's sleeping on the couch time, big boy.

Men, if you're getting the impression that this "thing" you must do is difficult, you're right. Before getting on the train, *your job is to listen to the woman express herself and help her feel understood.*

Listening to her and communicating understanding is the critical first part of the conversation—the "thing" you must do. It sets up the whole process! When the woman feels understood on the station platform, you'll get a nice send-off and a warm reception when you return. The conversation is off and running!

Men who learn this skill have better conversations with their wives. And because they have better conversations, they have happier wives and better marriages. And their needs are met by their happier wives. But the men who don't learn this skill. . .well, it'll be the flannel nightgown and the mean look every day of their miserable lives. So, the stakes are high, men. It's the bottom of the ninth. The winning run is on third base. Two out, three and two count. You need to hit the ball cleanly. You need to come through in the clutch.

For a man, listening to the woman and communicating understanding are extremely difficult to do. Like everything else in communication, these do not come naturally. It's difficult because of another major difference between the brains of men and women.

THE LOGICAL MAN

Men primarily operate logically. Our first reaction to most situations is logical:

"Give me the facts."

"What are the pros and cons?"

"Let's think rationally."

"Let's define the problem."

"Here are the possible solutions."

It is an impersonal, objective, intellectual reaction. No emotion is necessary. In fact, emotion just gets in the way and confuses things. Pure, beautiful logic keeps the mind clear and leads to the right decisions, based on what we can see, and observe, and measure. Everything else is fluff— froufrou. Unnecessary and irritating clutter. If it makes sense logically, then it makes sense.

We are calm, detached scientists applying rigorous and precise logic to every situation. It is a slow, step-by-step, methodical approach handed down from father to son for generations. A plus B plus C must equal D.

Men do have an emotional reaction, but it is secondary. We aren't even aware of our emotions until later in the conversation. We have to hop the train to find them.

THE EMOTIONAL WOMAN

Women primarily operate. . .guess how? Emotionally. A woman's first reaction to most situations is emotional:

"I'm angry. . .sad. . .frustrated. . .happy."

"Here's what each detail means to me."

"I'm upset, and I don't know why yet."

"I'm sensing. I'm going by feel."

It is a personal, more subjective, gut-level reaction. A woman automatically attaches herself to a situation and reacts emotionally to every detail in that situation. She notices and responds to every nuance, subtlety, and shade of gray. Body language, bad breath, the crack in the ceiling, and the song playing on the radio—everything passes through her emotional grid.

She's a sensitive, touchy-feely artist using all her senses at the same time to assess a situation. She sees, she hears, she touches, she tastes, and she smells. And most of all, she feels. She's trying to get a feeling for the situation.

It is a rapid-fire, unpredictable, shoot-from-the-hip (and the mouth) approach that the women in her life taught her to use. There is no particular order or sequence to her emotional reaction. She just lets it happen:

"There's definitely A. And I guess there's T. Yeah, yeah, T's good. Maybe F, but I'm not sure. Wait, something's coming in. Yes. Q. Here's Q. W is definitely a problem. I hate W. I have no idea how it all adds up. I'm still working my way through the alphabet."

All of her emotional reactions, senses, and impressions are channeled into her intuition. There is such a thing as a woman's intuition. It's real and it works. It works because the woman is aware of so much more in a situation than a man. She picks up things—sometimes critical, small details—that he misses completely.

A woman's first reaction to an event or situation is almost purely emotional. That's how she's made by God. She does have a logical reaction, but it is secondary. She can be just as logical as the man, but that won't happen until later in the conversation. She'll have to ride her own train to find the logic.

When a couple buys a car or sells their house, this logical-emotional difference is clearly in evidence. The man's first reaction to the car is airtight logic: "Does this car meet my checklist of requirements? Does it have the room, the options, the miles per gallon, the good maintenance record, the resale value, and the right price?"

Forget emotion. He won't allow himself to get excited before there's a real possibility he'll buy it. Now, after the car has met his logical standards, he can let his emotions out to play. "Hey, this baby does look sharp. It's the kind of car a guy like me would drive."

The woman's first reaction to the car is pure emotion. "Oh, look at this one. It's so pretty! It's so cute! I've always loved the color green. I really love this car." She immediately bonds with the car emotionally. She "feels" good about it. Or, she doesn't feel good about it—immediately. "I hate this car. It's ugly. It gives me the creeps. I wouldn't drive this car if it were the last one on earth."

After her initial burst of emotion, she will move to the logical level and consider the car's features and options. But she won't be logical until she feels good about the car. First, she and the car become friends. Then, she'll decide if the car's features allow their relationship to continue. If not, she'll grieve the loss quickly and move on to the next car.

When a man and his wife sell their house, again they react differently. The woman is losing a very good friend and wants to make sure it will be in good hands. She'll say: "I feel good about the Smith family. They love this home like I do, and they'll take care of it." The man could care less if the Smith family will take care of the home. He's only concerned, initially, about the deal. "I don't care if the Smiths are a group of serial killers, as long as I get my price."

Later on in the process, the man and woman get to their secondary reactions. Once the woman feels good about the Smiths, she'll look at the money part of the deal. Once the man gets the deal he wants, he might emotionally consider who's buying the house and how they'll take care of it.

This difference in how the sexes initially react in situations causes all kinds of trouble in conversation. Most women don't move to the logical level because the conversation does not last long enough. It's over before she can make the transition from emotion to logic. It's also over before any intimacy can happen. Not surprisingly, the unwitting culprit in many of these abbreviated conversations is the man. He short-circuits talk after talk and doesn't even know he's doing it. The problem is, he can't yet deal effectively with an emotional woman.

This is partly because most conversations begin with the woman talking. That's okay. She talks more. She's more expressive. When she begins talking, very often she will be on the emotional level. If it's a personal issue, there is a 100 percent guarantee she'll be on the emotional level. She'll be expressing her emotions. She'll be responding to all the details of a situation. She'll be bringing out her gut reaction. She'll also be freaking out the man.

All her emotion throws the man off balance because he's on the logical level. He naturally responds to her logically. This is a mistake. It isn't a malicious mistake. He's not trying to hurt the woman, but he does. So many, many conversations end this way! The woman is emotional. The man responds logically. No connection. No conversation. Plenty of frustration, resentment, and hurt feelings.

Let's take a look at how this problem operates in conversations. You need to know how *not* to do it before you can learn how to do it right.

FOURTEEN

HOW TO KILL A CONVERSATION

I had a crazy dream the other night. I dreamed that two television stars from the sixties, Jack Webb and Lucille Ball, got married. Jack was still in character as Joe Friday, the terminally serious police detective in *Dragnet*. Lucille was still playing her zany Lucy Ricardo role from *I Love Lucy*. In my dream, Joe and Lucy decided on their honeymoon to star in their own television show. It was called "Joe Loves Lucy."

JOE FRIDAY
LOVES LUCY RICARDO

You remember Joe Friday in *Dragnet*. The ultimate, no-nonsense, by the book, my collar is too tight, stick of a man—Mr. Logic himself. Joe relied on his intellectual reasoning to solve every problem in his work and life. Of course, he had no life except his work. He spoke only the words that needed to be spoken. He found humor unnecessary. He found smiling unnecessary.

Joe's famous motto, the one he uttered about ten times on each show, was: "Just give me the facts, nothing but the facts." If Joe could get the facts, he could solve the crime. If Joe could get the facts, he could decide whether to get the cheeseburger or the ham on rye for lunch.

Emotions, for Joe, were nothing but the silly, confused ramblings of weak individuals. Joe didn't have emotions, and he was disgusted with persons who broke down and expressed their emotions. And Joe especially couldn't tolerate emotions in women. His job forced him to deal with women in crisis situations, but he didn't like it. When a woman he was interviewing got too emotional, Joe would immediately try to shut down her sniveling and get her to be rational by saying something like: "Yes, I know your son was cut to pieces by a buzz saw right in front of you. Tough way to go. But crying won't bring Timmy back. Just give me the facts, ma'am, stick to the facts. Where do you think Timmy's right foot ended up?"

In *I Love Lucy*, Lucy Ricardo's personality and approach to life were just a tiny shade different from Joe's. Lucy was a zany, crazy, unpredictable, and intense woman. She bounced from one madcap adventure to another, usually in the company of her best friend and neighbor, Ethel.

Lucy never had an emotion she didn't share. Anything she felt, she expressed spontaneously in a loud, shrill voice. And she felt a lot of emotions. She screamed, laughed, and cried her way through every show. When a crisis hit, Lucy didn't sit down and think about what to do. She just reacted and let her emotions run wild. She would do whatever her emotions drove her to do.

Logic was definitely not Lucy's strength. She wouldn't listen to reason. She'd ignore rational advice from others, including Ethel, and keep making a bigger and bigger mess of things. Eventually Ricky Ricardo, her bandleader husband, would discover all the mayhem and destruction Lucy had caused. In his thick Latin accent, Ricky would yell: "Lucy! You got some 'splaining to do!" Finally, at the end of the show, Lucy would calm down and talk Ricky through her latest caper. Ricky wouldn't totally understand her, but he'd forgive her, and the show would close on a happy, harmonious note.

Back to my dream. Joe Friday and Lucy Ricardo settled down together but did not live happily ever after. They didn't exactly have a marriage made in heaven. Put bluntly, their relationship was a disaster. Lucy's high-octane emotional outbursts drove poor, logical Joe nuts.

They were never able to finish a conversation! Lucy would be all emotional and worked up as she talked to Joe. Joe would continually interrupt and try to get her to calm down. He kept saying in his classic monotone voice: "Lucy, you're not making any sense. Your emotion is clouding your mind. Just give me the facts." His logical approach infuriated Lucy, and she'd get even more upset, loud, and emotional.

Finally, Joe had enough, and he put the cuffs on her. He

handcuffed her to the dining-room table and walked out of the house. (In my dream, the men in the studio audience stood up and cheered at this point.) Lucy yelled after him: "You'll never understand me, you big ox! Why can't you just listen? Things always worked out with Ricky." The women in the studio audience rushed to her aid and tried to get her handcuffs off. That's when I woke up in a cold sweat.

Can you imagine what a marriage between Joe Friday and Lucy Ricardo would be like? Of course you can. You're living it. You have a Joe Friday-Lucy Ricardo marriage, don't you? If it isn't exactly like Joe and Lucy, it's close enough. Don't deny it. Don't feel too badly about it, either. I have one, too.

Almost all marriages have a Mr. Impeccable Logic and a Mrs. Raw Emotion. It's a tough combination. All of us Joe Fridays make the same mistake over and over and over. We respond logically to an emotional woman. It doesn't work, and we end up making a bigger mess than Lucy ever made.

Here are four common logical responses men are famous for making to a woman who is emotional. I've been guilty of every one of these. Men, let's learn from these mistakes.

"YOU SHOULDN'T FEEL THAT WAY"

The woman is being emotional and expressing herself with the man. Her feelings may be directed at the man for something he's done or said. Or, she may be venting feelings about another person or situation in her life. She's open. She's honest. She's sharing her heart with the man she loves.

The man assesses what he's hearing and decides he can save the woman a lot of time and hassle. He says, in so many words: "Hey, there's no need to react emotionally under these circumstances. So, don't. Stop feeling!"

This is a crude attempt to talk the woman out of her feelings. He sees no logical reason for her to be experiencing feelings. Once she understands there is no basis for her emotions, she can shut them down. Right? I'm afraid not. The woman isn't wrong to react emotionally. That's how she's made! It is an integral part of her nature. It is part of what makes her a woman. It is natural and healthy. (I've tried this "stop feeling" approach on my wife, Sandy, many times, and it just doesn't work.)

Sandy will be angry and hurt because of something I did. She'll spray these feelings all over me. It's like being soaked with a high-pressure fire hose. As she's emoting, I realize with a spark of hope that her whole argument has no foundation. She has misunderstood me! She has misinterpreted the whole situation! I "didn't mean to" upset her. I am an innocent man because my motivation was pure. No jury in the world would convict me.

It's too bad I'm not in front of a jury. I might have a chance. I'm in front of Sandy, and she doesn't appreciate my effort to take away her emotions. I explain her misinterpretation. I explain that I didn't mean to cause her pain, and I honestly expect Sandy to realize her mistake and feel better right away. I'd love for her to say, just once: "Oh, I guess I had it all wrong. As long as you didn't mean to, I don't have to be angry and hurt."

I'm still waiting for Sandy to say words like these. What happens is, she gets even angrier because I'm trying to explain away her feelings. Whether I meant to upset her is not the issue. She is upset and is entitled to her feelings.

Women are sensitive. They are affected by events on a

deeper level than men. My Sandy, and almost all women, reach a pretty high level of emotional intensity in a very brief period of time. We're talking nanoseconds here. And it takes women awhile, typically an hour or more, to "come down" emotionally from their peak of intensity. It will take them even longer if you offer some brilliant, logical explanation of why they shouldn't even have emotions.

Another way we men try to shut down a woman's emotions is to jump in and say: "I'm sorry." We're not really sorry. We just want you to stop the emotional barrage. We're running up the white flag in a desperate ploy to save ourselves from more emotional missiles. If you keep firing, we say in an exasperated and self-righteous tone: "Look, I said I was sorry. What more do you want?"

What she wants, and needs, is to be listened to and heard. Sorry is nice, and it might even help, after she has vented and feels like the man has understood her emotions.

"Why Are You So Upset?"

This response is a little more clever than the previous one. Here, the man can see the need for some emotion. As the woman talks, even he has to admit that in these circumstances, any reasonable person would be emotional. So he says to her: "I don't blame you for being upset, honey. I did run over Twinkles the cat with my car." Or: "Boy, that is rough. Too bad your friend's house burned down."

The catch is, he thinks she's overreacting. A certain amount of emotion is okay, but she's going over the line. He tells her that her emotions are too intense.

"You're too upset, Betty."

"This is overkill, honey."

"Get a grip on yourself."

"Calm down, will you?"

This approach works like a charm. The woman hears his wise counsel and immediately realizes her emotions are too intense and not appropriate for the situation. With some embarrassment, she apologizes. "You're right, sweetheart. Thanks for your feedback. I guess I got a little carried away. Is this calmer now?"

Men, if you thought she was too intense before, just wait until you lay this logical approach on her. You ain't seen intense. She'll be offended and just plain mad at your nerve in telling her she has too much emotion.

Listen, men. The woman is not on the logical level yet, so her emotions can be pretty raw. She is, by nature, more emotionally intense than you will ever be. She's not out of control. She's not crazy or unstable. She won't kill people or run over small animals. Her feelings are very strong and somewhat ragged, particularly as she begins talking. But she does *not* have too much emotion.

Men, I know you don't know how to handle the intensity of the woman's emotions. You think she's out of control. You think she's irrational. So, you try to get her to regain control by asking her to lower the intensity of her emotions. Ever throw gasoline on an open fire? That's what it's like when you try to calm the woman down. You turn a small brush fire into a raging inferno.

If you want a woman to calm down, you've got to learn how to maintain your poise when she is emotionally intense. She's okay. She's just fine. Really. She will calm down, if you patiently let her do her thing. Let her go. Let her be intense. Don't interrupt a woman when she's on a roll, unless you want to suffer! Allow her to back up her emotional dump truck and completely dump her load of emotions all over you. She'll clean her system and eventually come down to an emotional level you can deal with more comfortably.

"THAT'S LIFE, SWEETHEART"

The woman begins to talk about an event that has occurred in her life. The event may or may not have involved the man. As she cranks up her emotional volume and warms to the story's details, Mr. Logic steps in and stops her dead in her tracks using the classic "That's life, sweetheart" method to abruptly cut off the conversation. He says to her, with a straight face: "Hey, the past is the past. It happened, and there's nothing we can do about it now. It's ancient history. Let's move on, shall we?"

This is such a compassionate and caring approach, isn't it? He's actually doing her a favor. If the past is gone and can't be addressed, then she can save herself the trouble and pain of expressing about it. All she has to do is what he does: say it's over and done with, block it out of her mind, and stride with confidence into the future.

This approach is great for combat situations. When the allied forces were storming the beach at Normandy, there was no time to stop and grieve the dead. "They got Fred. His head's blown off! Henry! Oh, no! Henry's down!" If you paused to express your feelings, you'd be killed on the beach. You just had to suck it up and move on, or you didn't make it. So men, when you're in an actual combat situation, feel free to forget the past and move ahead. But when your wife is upset and expressing herself, this approach doesn't work. In fact, it's a disaster!

You try it with your wife, and you might find yourself in a combat situation like this one: A young mother was in my therapy office with her husband. She was struggling to adjust to all the changes her first child, a newborn, had brought into her life. She shared deeply for ten minutes how hard it was being a new mom. The baby's constant needs. Lack of sleep. Fatigue. No life of her own.

When she was finished, she looked expectantly at her husband. He responded in a voice heavy with sarcasm: "Well, welcome to motherhood!" Not exactly what she wanted to hear. I had to pry her hands off his scrawny little throat! This lady wanted and needed her pain to be heard, some understanding, and some help with the baby. What she got was: "That's life, sweetheart. Get over it."

"Stand Back, Little Lady, Daddy's Gonna Help"

As the woman launches into her emotional description of an event, the man instantly sees it as a problem. And he is the problem solver. He cuts her off and goes into his answer-man mode: "Honey, I see your problem. I have good news. I can fix it for you. Now, here's what I would do if I were you." He gives her a logical, rational, five-point plan of action. He is so sure his advice will help make her feel better. That is because when he has a plan, he feels better.

The woman beams at her Mr. Fix-It and gushes: "Oh, happy day! You've given me a plan, and now I don't have to feel so crummy. Why, my nasty feelings are all gone." Not quite. Instead, she feels rejected and insulted!

Another variation of the "Daddy's Gonna Help" approach is the man telling the woman a story about his own life. He thinks that if he tells her his story, she won't feel so alone and may pick up some ideas on how to solve her problem. He says, "You know, honey, that reminds me of the time I was in Cleveland, and a similar thing happened to me. . ." He means well, but he is wrong! This may help another man, but it won't do anything for the woman.

Men, providing a logical solution is not what the woman wants or needs. She's looking for a connection, some closeness, and understanding. She wants you to fix the appliances, but not her personal problems. At least, not right away. Now if she comes up and says right to your face: "Honey, help me fix this problem now. Give me your logical plan." Then, go for it! If not, let her talk, and you just listen.

Men, all these logical responses slam the conversation into a brick wall. Your logic, instead of bringing order and rationality to the situation, causes chaos and even more emotion to erupt from the woman. You don't mean to produce this kind of trouble, but you do.

It's important for both sexes to understand why men respond logically to an emotional woman. I've already covered some of the reasons. But there are several underlying reasons that are the key to the male logical response system. When these are understood, logic can be put in its proper place in a conversation. And when that happens, a conversation has a chance to move toward intimacy.

FIFTEEN

CAPTAIN KIRK MEETS HIS MATCH

A lone figure stands on the surface of a small, uncharted planet deep in the Gamma Twenty solar system. Star Date 353.4851. The figure is none other than James T. Kirk, captain of the starship, USS *Enterprise*. He is alone because the transporter system of the *Enterprise* failed, and his four crewmen didn't materialize. (That dumb transporter is always malfunctioning.)

Captain Kirk has come to this obscure planet on the orders of Star Fleet Command. There are sketchy reports that a strange and hideous alien lives here, guarding a priceless treasure of mineral deposits. Kirk's mission is to build a good relationship with the alien and secure the mineral rights. Countless other men have tried to establish contact with the alien, but all have failed. Typical of men, they have never talked about it.

Captain Kirk is well suited to this important task. His courage and toughness are well known throughout the universe. Through seventy-nine episodes on the *Star Trek* television series and six major motion pictures, Kirk has proven his worth as a fearless and cunning negotiator with all kinds of aliens.

He has almost always won the confidence of the aliens he's come up against on the field of battle. If he hasn't been able to make friends with an alien, he's just killed it. Whatever the result, Kirk has come out on top every time. But this time, will Kirk meet his match?

The confrontation, when it comes, is surprisingly short. The alien appears, and Kirk is amazed at its beauty and charm. He doesn't understand what it's saying, but he's attracted to it strongly. (Of course, Kirk is attracted to every female life form he sees.) Then the interaction begins to get a little tense. The alien becomes frustrated because it cannot make Kirk understand its language. Kirk tries the universal translator, a gizmo that compares brain waves and frequencies. Even that doesn't work.

Suddenly, the alien changes from a beautiful creature to a horrible, grotesque monster. Its whole demeanor and mood become incredibly intense. The volume and rate of its speech reach astronomical levels.

Captain Kirk tries to stop the creature from spinning out of control. His attempts to reason with it fail miserably. In fact, every word he says seems to enrage the alien further.

Shaking and frothing at the mouth, the creature's anger and intensity continue to escalate.

Kirk is shocked by the awesome power emanating from inside the alien. Despite its small size, it terrifies him. For the first time in his career, he has no idea what to do. Completely overwhelmed, he uses the oldest trick in the book. He shouts: "Look out behind you!" When the monster turns to look, Kirk runs away like a coward.

This is not just some science fiction fantasy. Oh, no. I have just described what it's like for a man to face a woman who is expressing her emotions. Yes, ladies, it's that bad. Really.

Most women have no idea of the shattering impact their emotional intensity has on a man. He may not show much on the outside, but inside he's cringing. Her intensity scares him. Nauseates him. Confuses him. Angers him. He'll do anything to stop it or at least, reduce it. If all else fails, like Captain Kirk, he'll get out of there!

Why Men Avoid Emotion

There are three key underlying reasons why men continue stubbornly to use logic in response to a woman who is emotional. Maybe these aren't good reasons, but they are the truth. Let's take a look at the shaky foundation of male logic.

Logic Is the Answer

The first reason is, we really think logic is best. We really do. Logic is the answer to all of life's events and problems.

There isn't anything life can throw at you that can't be handled with logic.

We operate most of the time on the logical level. We're comfortable there. Logic is safe. Secure. It has organization. There are rational steps to take. Oh, and logic helps us stay in control (remember Chapters Two and Three?).

We hate—absolutely hate—situations in which we feel out of control. And that's the main problem we have with emotion. For us, emotion equals being out of control. Emotion is so. . .so. . .so. . .chaotic! So unpredictable! Anything can happen, and it usually does.

When we're with an emotionally intense woman, we don't know what she's going to say or do. She's firing in all different directions. (The scary part is, she doesn't even know what she's going to say next!) We don't know what's around the next corner. It's like being on Mr. Toad's Wild Ride for the first time. She's definitely out of control, and that makes us feel out of control. Using logic, we can try to steady her and give her control. Even if that doesn't work, logic will keep us in control.

Some emotion is fine. Sure. We have emotions, and it's okay for the woman to have emotions. As long as those emotions aren't too personal, or too deep, or too intense. Emotions need to be low-level and under control. Don't get too excited because when emotion crosses a certain threshold, it's trouble. The whole atmosphere is immediately charged with electricity. It's like being caught in the open in a violent lightning storm. If we don't take cover, we're going to get zapped. Logic is our cover.

FORGET THE PAST

Second, we hate emotion because it usually drives the woman to talk about the past. If there's one thing we can't stand, it's the woman bringing up some old thing and going over it again. I touched on this in the previous chapter, but let's get a little deeper.

Men are geared to focus on the present and the future. We have poor memories and can't recall what happened ten minutes ago, let alone ten years ago. But it's more than that. We automatically erase the past (or try to) and look forward. Yesterday is gone. It's over. We can't change the past. We can do something today and tomorrow and next week. New, fresh challenges are what we want.

The past is meaningless to us. Trivial. Dead. Buried. Please, don't dig it up. Let it stay back there. For men, talking about the past is like turning the car around and going back and picking up roadkill. And then being forced to eat it for dinner.

Men, I know how you feel. I used to feel the same way. Recently, with Sandy's help, I have come to realize the value of talking about the past. I still look forward. That's a good trait to have. But now I'm better at dealing with past events.

Let me illustrate how important this is: A lady and her husband were in my office. We were a couple of weeks into marital therapy and had just hit a major issue. The woman shared that, years ago when they were just married, she had had an abortion. She sobbed as she told the story. They had no money. He was in school. They didn't think they could afford a child and didn't feel ready to be parents. "So," she whispered, "I went to a clinic and had my baby killed." Her guilt and pain were overwhelming, even after all the years.

Her husband listened to the story in stoic silence. He seemed cold, detached, and unable to connect with her emotions. He said in a flat tone: "Look, it happened. It was wrong. I feel forgiven. It's over with. I don't want to talk about it anymore."

He didn't realize the key to healing his marriage was talking about the abortion. I forced him to face it and, in the long run, he thanked me. He had emotions about the abortion, all right. He was just using logic to block them. It was hurting him, because he continued to carry his own guilt and shame and loss from the abortion. It was hurting his wife, because he stubbornly refused to allow her to vent her tremendous pain. And, of course, his logic was hurting his marriage. They were two hurting persons unable to talk honestly about the most significant trauma in their lives.

When they expressed their emotions and grieved this loss together, everything changed. They could feel, for the first time, God's forgiveness. They felt like a great burden had been lifted from their individual lives and from their marriage. They cleaned out resentments and genuinely connected on a deep level. All because the man decided, with some urging by me and my cattle prod, to go back and deal with the past.

He tried to convince me that the past, especially the abortion, wasn't an issue. I asked him three questions. "Why are you so dissatisfied with your life? Why is your wife so depressed? Why is your marriage so unhappy and empty of passion?" He had no answers.

I told him: "I know why. It's because you haven't talked about the past! You two haven't been the same since the abortion. When you talk it through, you'll get better."

My final point to this man was, in the end, the one that

sold him on dealing with the past. I said: "If you love your wife, let her express her emotions about the past." I explained to him that a woman must talk about things that have happened to her, particularly painful things. She needs to understand what has happened. She needs to assess the impact on her life. She needs to get her emotions out, or they will bottle up inside and damage her emotionally and physically.

This man did love his wife and didn't want to damage her. He forced himself to let her talk about the past. He shelved his logic and ended up with a happy wife and a better marriage.

I went on to explain to him that if you eliminate the past from conversation, there isn't much to talk about! More serious traumas certainly have to be addressed verbally, but so do a lot of other past events. Let's face it, you can't talk about the present because it's still happening. You can't talk too deeply about the future because it hasn't happened yet. Ninety-nine percent of deep, intimate conversations are about the past!

When you do it the right way, both partners share what they think happened. Their emotions. Their motivations. Their unique views of the event. How they think God is guiding them through the event. What they can learn about each other because of what happened. Couples who talk like this, about the past, are the couples who achieve intimacy.

EMOTIONS MEAN NO CONTROL

The third reason men avoid the emotions of women is that we desperately want to steer clear of our own emotions. We're extremely uncomfortable with personal emotions, especially painful ones. When these kinds of deep emotions start coming up inside, we feel naked. Unprotected. Exposed. We think we will completely lose control and end up blubbering, pathetic eunuchs.

We've noticed that our own deeper emotions tend to surface when the woman is expressing her emotions. If we really listen to her and try to understand, guess what will happen? We'll get emotional, too! We'll feel. And we don't want that. We need to stop her, and fast. Logic will do the trick. We'd rather have her be furious at us for using logic. This distracts her and keeps us from connecting with our emotions. It makes for a long night, but anything's better than losing control and becoming emotional. We keep our tough exterior up and show her nothing. She'll beat against our tough clamshell with her crowbar, but she won't get inside.

Men, it's time to drop the tough guy act. Being tough will get you nowhere. It also gets your marriage nowhere. That's for sure. There can be no intimacy when you hide behind your wall, your clamshell of toughness.

There are a few things toughness will get you. Loneliness, a stale marriage, and an early death. You think I'm kidding? Take a look at Humphrey Bogart and John Wayne. Two quintessential tough guys, in the movies and in real life. Just read about their lives. Go ahead. Fame. Money. Power. Broken marriages. Neglected kids. Unhappiness. Addictions. Premature deaths. Not too pretty. In fact, downright depressing. Bogie and the Duke were both workaholics and nicotine addicts. Both died of cancer. They killed themselves with toughness. But hey, they were tough. You've got to give Bogie and the Duke that.

Men, if you stay tough, you don't get rid of your feelings. They remain and fester inside. They have to be released.

They have to go somewhere. And they will. They'll go into an addiction. Not maybe. They will.

Here's a list. Take your pick.

Smoking

Drinking

Drugs

Sex

Work

Gambling

Eating

Sports

You don't have to pick, do you? Chances are, you have one of these addictions right now. Or, you're well on your way to developing one. Any one of these addictions will damage you and your marriage. You don't want to be addicted, but your stuffed emotions must go somewhere.

I know what I'm talking about. I spent years of my marriage holding back my emotions from Sandy.

In 1982, while at Dallas Seminary, I went through a very stressful period. I had been on track to become a Christian psychologist. That was the plan. Sandy and I both were working toward this goal. Then, I encountered my first group therapy sessions—as a chaplain/counselor, not as a patient. The pain and misery I heard in those early groups freaked me out so much that I had second thoughts about psychology. I began to consider youth ministry. I even made some appointments to talk to Dallas professors about my future.

I played the tough guy and told Sandy nothing.

I was stressed out of my mind. I wasn't sleeping well. I even had heart palpitations. Sandy knew something was wrong and asked me repeatedly what was going on. Guess what I said? That's right. "Nothing." I wanted to handle it on my own.

Finally, I realized I had to talk to Sandy. I had to risk being vulnerable and show her my deeper emotions. After all, she was (and is) my best friend. I talked and shared and expressed my emotions. My fears. My stress. My confusion.

Boy, did I feel better. I could sleep again. My stress level went back to normal. My heart went back to normal. And my marriage got better. Sandy and I were closer than we had ever been. Plus, after we had connected emotionally and she assured me of her love and support, Sandy gave me her objective opinion. It went something like this: "Be a youth pastor if you want. But I think you're crazy. That's not your gift. You'd make a much better Christian psychologist." As she has been so often, Sandy was right.

You can stay tough with everybody else in your life—customers, coworkers, neighbors, family, and friends. It's okay to be tough and strong and logical. There's a place for this. In a crisis or some other situation that calls for leadership, these traits come in handy. But don't do it with your dear wife, your best friend, your lover. With her, you need to drop the tough guy act. Be honest, be real, be open to emotion (hers and yours) in personal conversations with her. You won't regret it.

THE RESULTS OF LOGIC

Driven by these three reasons, the man tries to force-feed logic to his wife.

The four logical responses described in Chapter Fourteen are all attempts by the man to shut down the woman's emotional reaction and get her to join him on the logical level. But the woman can't suddenly move to the logical level. She's wired to respond emotionally first. (There are a few women who respond with logic first, but not many.)

Eventually, she will be logical. But it'll be a little while. So the conversation gets stuck. No deeper level can be reached. It becomes a power struggle. The man tries to get the woman to be logical and she becomes even more emotional and, finally, the conversation dead-ends. The man ends up feeling frustrated: "Women! Who can figure them out?" The woman ends up feeling rejected and misunderstood: "Men! What a bunch of clods!"

The result: Unwittingly, the man creates a mess.

A Man's Gotta Do
What a Man's Gotta Do

Listen, men. The woman has to put up with us getting on the train. The least we can do is learn how to listen to her and help her feel understood when she's emotional. Fair is fair.

If the woman does not feel understood, you've got trouble. She feels rejected. She'll either push for a response or back away from you. She'll become the Great Nag of the North or the Ice Queen. Either way, you lose. But if the woman feels understood, a lot of nice conversational things happen. She'll feel loved by you. She'll let you use the train and be ready to continue the conversation when you return. It buys you time for the train!

Also, by listening, you start your train trip. You begin,

right there on the platform, getting in touch with your emotions. You need more time to identify and bring out your emotions. But you can kick off the process when she's talking and expressing her emotions because you need the woman to trigger your emotions. God made her to go over and over events in an emotional way so you can finally catch on and get in touch with your own emotions. This is what God wants to happen on the train platform! It's part of His plan for opposite-sex communication. And His plan is always the best plan.

SIXTEEN

BETTER SAFE THAN SORRY

A man has a one-track mind. (No, I'm not talking about sex.) I'm referring to a man's tendency to believe he has the truth in every situation in life. He has thought about the situation. He has considered all the options. He has objectively applied his logic. He has carefully processed the available facts. Therefore, it follows that his conclusion is the best conclusion. His way is the best way. He is right and you, the woman, are wrong.

He doesn't want you to take it personally. He's not being selfish or malicious about it. He really believes he has found the truth. On his own, without any help from anyone, he has come to the one conclusion that makes sense in these circumstances. His version of an event must be correct. It just must be.

A woman has, by nature, a two-track mind. She can consider not just her version of a situation but also the man's version. She can accept what he is saying and try to somehow reconcile his truth and her truth. She can more easily compromise, negotiate, and find a middle ground.

A man, by nature, considers only what he thinks and feels. His position, which he worked hard to develop, is the only position to hold. He doesn't see any middle ground. No offense intended, but he sees himself and his view occupying the high ground.

"HERE ARE THE STONE TABLETS, HONEY"

When a man comes down from the mountain and hands the woman his decision on the stone tablets, he actually expects her to uncritically accept it. In fact, he thinks she ought to be grateful. He has given her the truth. "Oh, thank you, great swami, for these tablets on which is engraved ultimate truth."

When the woman tries to share her view and her feelings about a situation, he's offended. You see, her view isn't necessary. He's already delivered the one true view. Can't she see that?

A man was in my office, sitting next to his wife on the couch. (Clients usually sit on my couch, not lie on it.) He said to me in a very authoritative voice: "I do love my wife. Of course, I do. If I say I do, then I do."

I replied: "That's what you say. That's fine. Thanks for sharing. Now let's see what your wife says."

His wife said: "I don't feel loved by you, Harry. I haven't felt loved for three years."

I said to Harry: "Harry, listen to her. If she says you don't love her, you don't love her. You must use her definition and not just yours."

Harry put up a fight, but in the end he realized that he had to use his wife's definition of love. He honestly thought he was loving her, but he was honestly wrong. Since she is the object of his love, she would be the one to know if she's loved. Right? Right. I explained to Harry that, from now on, he needed to ask his wife regularly if she felt loved. He needed to ask her regularly if her needs were being met. Her responses would be his guide.

I had another couple in my office. In their session the previous week, they had mentioned a big decision they had to make in the next few weeks. In this week's session, the man presented his decision on this issue—his stone tablets of truth. As he spoke, it became quickly apparent that he had not consulted his wife at all in his decision-making process. On his own, he had carefully deliberated and come up with what he thought was the best plan. Classic male thinking.

What did I say to him? I said: "That's what you say. That's fine. Thanks for sharing. Now let's see what your wife says." She was, of course, insulted and hurt because he hadn't asked for her input on the decision.

She said: "Pete, please involve me in the decision. Am I your wife or the housekeeper? Don't you need my view, my opinion, on this?"

Pete, like a lot of husbands, didn't realize he was cutting his wife out of the conversational equation over and over again. His inability to consider his wife's position on issues was a huge conversation-stopper in their relationship.

Men, when you stop conversations, you stop the marriage. It's okay to have your view on an issue. It's okay to use logic to come up with it. Just don't think your view is the best and only view. It's only half of the equation. You're married. Remember that beautiful lady who lives with you? What she says and thinks and feels is just as important as your position in every conversation.

Male-female conversations are very fragile things. As a conversation starts, it is just barely alive. It's like a baby Kemp's ridley sea turtle freshly hatched on the beach who must crawl thirty to forty yards to the sea with no protection. It is the most dangerous and risky time in the turtle's life. If it can just make the water without being picked off by a predator, its chances of survival go up. Even after it gets to the sea, the turtle must still face a host of predators and other threats to its life.

Kemp's ridley sea turtles, like all sea turtles, are an endangered species. Some research indicates one in a thousand baby sea turtles makes it all the way to adulthood.

Your conversations, like these sea turtles, are an endangered species. They are incredibly vulnerable when they are just born. They remain vulnerable throughout their life span (which, as you recall from Chapter Eleven, ought to be at least several days). Don't take chances! Don't take risks! Play it safe and carefully nurture your conversations along. Give them a chance to grow and develop.

Here are some basic guidelines to safely move your conversations to a deeper level. You can, by working together, do a whole lot better than one good conversation in a thousand. I have two safety instructions for men, and two for women.

LEARN TO LISTEN AND REFLECT

When the woman is talking there on the train platform, a man's job is to listen and reflect. It's the safest and best approach with a woman who is on the emotional level. Make sure she knows you're listening. Don't assume she knows. Make it obvious. Establish and maintain eye contact, unless you're driving a car. Sit close to her, not across the room. Don't do anything in addition to listening. No television. No radio. No computer. No newspaper. No book. No answering the phone. You are a man, and you cannot do two things at the same time. Listening to your woman isn't easy and will require all your concentration.

While you are listening, only open your mouth to repeat and rephrase what she is saying. It's called reflection. You say nothing original! When she's talking and expressing herself, it's all about her. It's not about you. You can share your stuff—opinions, reactions, and thoughts—later. If you jump the gun and interrupt her with original material, there won't be a later.

Some men tell me: "But, Dave, my memory is bad. If I don't say what's on my mind right away, I forget it. Then, when it's my turn, I have nothing to say." I tell these men to use the pad (check Chapter Five again). As she's speaking, jot down what's coming into your head. Just don't say it out loud.

Men, creating understanding is your goal. This is a two-way street. You must understand what she is saying and feeling. Also, she must believe that you are understanding her, which you communicate by feeding back to her key words and key phrases she is using. Focus not just on content—what she is saying, but on emotion—*what she is feeling*. Feeding her these small pieces of content and emotion keeps the conversation on track. She knows you are right there with her. She'll be able to express more deeply and, when it's time for you to hop the train, she'll graciously let you go.

I hope you're getting the message: You don't just listen in silence. That's the kiss of death. When you are a silent listener, she'll think you're not listening. Guess what she'll do? She'll talk more! She talks enough as it is. You don't want more words, do you? The woman will just keep repeating what she's saying until she thinks you've heard and understood it. If you're like me, you really hate it when the woman goes over and over and over the same event. I mean, isn't once enough? *Once isn't enough if she's not sure you've understood it.*

Save yourself from being buried in a massive mudslide of repeated details. A woman will talk a lot and use numerous details the first time through. That's a woman. But, I'm telling you, you can reduce her output significantly with active listening and reflection. You really can control, to a degree, how long she talks and how many times she repeats herself.

This isn't just good communication. It's survival. If you're a passive, silent listener, and not reflecting back to a woman, she will go above your detail threshold. When that happens, your brain will register "full," and you'll stop listening. She'll notice, and you're toast.

If you're a smart listener and reflector, you'll check with the woman to make sure she feels you're understanding her. At regular intervals as she speaks, ask her: "Do you feel like I'm with you? Am I missing anything?" When she's finished her part of the conversation, ask again: "Do you feel understood?"

If you're not sure about something she's said, ask her to clarify it. If you're not sure about the emotions she's feeling, ask her to tell you what they are. You keep listening and reflecting and clarifying until the woman tells you she feels understood. Then, you have done your job. The train trip, which you've already begun by listening well, can now be completed on your own.

Let me illustrate a poor job of listening and reflection.

For four wonderful years I owned a Volvo station wagon. It was the car of my dreams. I've always loved Volvos. Big, powerful, well-built, and incredibly safe machines. I even like their unusual, rectangular appearance. Sandy, however, has never liked Volvos. I believe her comment, as we shopped for station wagons, was: "The Volvo is just a big, ugly box." But somehow, through clean living and God's grace, I got my way.

It was a great car. Safe, dependable, and ran like a top. We had plenty of room for the three girls in the backseat. Life was good. A man and his machine living in harmony and security.

Then, suddenly, everything changed. Sandy got pregnant, a little unexpectedly, with our fourth child. Okay, it was a lot unexpectedly. She informed me that my Volvo would have to go because it didn't have enough room for Number Four. I was crushed. I felt betrayed. I tried to argue, but it's tough to win an argument with a woman who is six months pregnant in August in Florida. I finally agreed to sell my Volvo and buy another car.

My depression lifted when I realized I could now buy the real car of my dreams. Volvos are great, but I had always wanted a Suburban. The ultimate man's car. A huge, indestructible, tank of a car. A big, honking, Godzilla of a car. I would literally own the road. I would eat small cars for breakfast.

I said nothing to Sandy at first, because she had made it clear she wanted a minivan. Oh, no! Not a minivan! That's a woman's car! Why, it's not even a real van! She gave me her special "look" and told me since I had chosen the Volvo, she should be able to choose the next car. It all came to a head one night in our bedroom when I finally got up the nerve to tell her I wanted to buy a Suburban. As soon as she heard the word Suburban, Sandy reacted with high emotional intensity. She said: "No! I hate Suburbans! They're trucks!"

I reacted immediately by telling her that a Suburban is not a truck, even though I knew it was. I rattled off with logical precision all the wonderful features of the Suburban. Sandy felt misunderstood, angry, and disgusted. The conversation did not go well.

My mistake, besides being crazy enough to even mention the Suburban, was not reflecting. When Sandy reacted emotionally, my job was to move into the listening and reflecting mode. That way, she would have calmed down eventually, and we could have had a decent conversation.

Technically, because I started the conversation, Sandy should have reflected. I didn't bother pointing that out to her. When a woman goes into emotional hyperdrive, the man must immediately shift gears and go into reflection mode.

By the way, guess what car we ended up buying? You know the answer, don't you? A minivan, of course. I have to admit, it has kind of grown on me.

TELL HER WHEN YOU'RE GETTING OVERWHELMED OR CONFUSED

You'll notice, men, I didn't say *if* you're getting overwhelmed or confused, I said *when*. It's very common to experience a brain short circuit as a woman talks. She uses a lot of words and, if that isn't enough of a challenge, she generates a sonic boom of intensity.

There are times when you simply can't process all the words. Your male mind just can't keep up. It's like a sumo wrestler chasing a world-class sprinter. "Excuse me, honey. I lost you back in paragraph three, sentence six." If her number of words doesn't get you, her emotional intensity will. A woman's intensity can turn a man's mind to mush. He can automatically raise his defensive shields, shut down, and lose his ability to listen.

Men, when you lose the woman in conversation, it is critically important to tell her immediately. Do not—I repeat, do not—try to fake your way through. It never works. You will not be a hero. You will be a goat. At the precise moment you are overwhelmed or confused, interrupt and tell her you've lost her. Say something like: "Sweetheart, you're blowing me out of the water. I lost you. Let's start over. I want to understand what you're saying."

You have a small window of opportunity from the time you've lost her to the time she realizes you've lost her. My research shows you have 1.4 seconds. If you don't tell her in that tiny window, she'll catch you zoning (remember Chapter Nine?). She'll see your glazed eyes—your "deer-in-the-headlights" look. She'll say: "Are you listening to me?" You'll say: "Sure. I'm right here with you, aren't I?" Then, she'll ask the question that pierces your soul and exposes you as a lying nonlistener: "What did I just say?"

The smell of burning toast will fill the room. You have triggered the domino effect. No, it has nothing to do with pizza. It refers to the rapid number of problems that spring up one right after the other. Problem Number One, you were not listening. Number Two, you lied about it. Three, the conversation is over. Four, the woman is angry and hurt. Five, you are in serious damage-control mode. And on and on.

She won't be happy when you interrupt to tell her you're lost, but at least she knows you're trying to understand her. Her minor irritation will pass quickly. And she won't mind repeating herself. That's her life. That's what she does!

Ask Up Front for a Listener

Ladies, some brief words for you.

First, it's important to make what you need clear to the man right up front. This is especially important when the two of you are learning these communication skills. A man does better when he has instructions and knows what's expected. Don't assume he knows. Don't hope he'll listen. That's too risky! Ask him, before you begin to talk, to be a listener. Telegraph it! Just come out and ask. "Honey, I have something personal/difficult/painful to discuss. Please just listen and help me feel understood."

Also, ladies, it's a good idea to make sure the man is in the optimal listening mode. If you start talking when he's occupied or distracted by any other activity it's like walking into a mine field. That's setting yourself up for failure, and it'll be your own fault. I have female clients talk to me about how their husbands can't listen to them if there's anything else going on in the immediate area. I tell each of these ladies: "Of course your husband can't. He's a man. If you talk to him when he's doing something else, you take your chances."

Men are highly distractible creatures. It doesn't take much to pull a man's attention away. If you're talking and the Braves score a run, a man's going to look at the television set!

So don't compete with any other activity. You'll lose. Ask a man to stop the activity. You can say: "Bob, I'd like to talk to you about something. I need your full attention. So, when you're ready to listen, please stop what you're doing and come to me."

TELL HIM WHEN HE'S BEING LOGICAL

Look, nobody's perfect, and a man will make mistakes as he learns how to listen to you. One of his most common mistakes will be slipping into a logical response. He's used to responding to you this way, so he will do it many times.

Interrupt him and get back on track. Don't let it pass, because if you do your resentment will build. Plus, without meaning to, he has effectively ended the conversation. Say to him: "Honey, that's a logical response, and I need listening right now." If he gets defensive, take a brief break for five or ten minutes. Then, restart the conversation.

It's a good idea to use this stop and restart method whenever a conversation gets off track, no matter the reason. Either partner can call for a break. You take five or ten, then come back and pick it up.

WHEN THE MAN SPEAKS FIRST

I have focused on conversations where the woman initiates because the woman initiates more than the man. And probably always will. That's okay. It's just the way it is.

There are times when the man initiates a conversation. It may happen in your lifetime, ladies. I mean, miracles do happen. Let's think positively. If a man uses his pad, he could very well start more talks. Here are a few guidelines when he does start the talking.

> Let him be logical. Since he's a man, he'll begin with logic. (That should not come as a huge shock to you.) It may bore you. It may be difficult to listen to him. Do it anyway.

> Fight your urge to drag him quickly to the emotional level. Don't say things like: "But, Bob, how do you feel? What's going on inside?" That's being a crowbar.

> Listen, reflect, and help him feel understood. That's your job. If he feels understood, chances are better that he'll be able to go deeper later on in the conversation. Pace yourself. Remember that a conversation will slowly develop over a number of days.

When he feels understood, then you get your turn to talk. That's when you can express emotionally. If you follow my plan, he will listen and reflect with you. Eventually, with the train, he can be emotional with you.

My basic rule of thumb is: Whoever starts a conversation gets to dictate the initial level. If the man starts, that means logic first. If the woman starts, that means emotion first. (If you men want to be logical more of the time, start more conversations.)

In any good conversation, a couple will hit both levels—logical and emotional—eventually. Logic is important. Decisions, deals, and compromises come when both partners are on the logical level.

Emotion is also important. I've focused on emotion because real depth and intimacy come only when both partners are on the emotional level.

MAW AND PAW
AT THE RANCH

A man and a woman meet, begin dating, fall in love, and get married. So far, so good. Their love is passionate and intense. They feel very close. They spend a lot of time together. The hours just fly by, and they never tire of each other's company. They talk for hours about all kinds of subjects. The words flow naturally and smoothly. The man and woman enjoy a vibrant, intense, physical relationship. They enjoy touching and kissing frequently. They have intercourse often, and it is spontaneous, playful, and fulfilling.

Several years after getting married, things begin to

change. Not all at once. But slowly, gradually, they drift apart. Day by day, week by week, their passion for each other drains away. They start looking outside the relationship to get their needs met.

She reads romance novels, cleans the house too often, and gets too involved with the children. If she works outside the home, she may focus on her career. She may spend too many hours a week in church or volunteer activities. She may develop several close female friendships and share more personal information with them than she does with her husband.

He works longer hours at his job and thinks about work even when he's home. He watches a lot of sports on television. He may golf on the weekends or get too involved in some other hobby. He plays computer games for hours at a time. He may begin flirting with women at the office. He may slide into a pattern of mental lust.

They spend very little time together. In fact, they avoid each other. Their conversations are awkward and stilted. There seem to be so many obstacles to emotional and physical intimacy. What used to be so easy is now difficult and painful. They don't know what to say to each other.

Oh, they still love each other. It's a concerned love, a caring love, but the kind between brother and sister or roommates. The fire is gone. The entire fireplace is gone. They are slowly boring each other to death. In the evenings, he watches television in the living room. She reads in the bedroom or talks on the phone. They don't really talk to each other anymore—just about the kids, the house, business matters. They still have sex, but it's not too often, and it's not too exciting. It's a brief act done to satisfy a biological urge. Real, tender touching is almost nonexistent.

Sound familiar? Many couples fit this same, sad scenario. Oh, you're still together, and that's good, but you're not too happy about it.

You used to have kisses that were wet smackers of excitement. Now, all you have are the brief, dry pecks of two persons who are just going through the motions. You've gone from passionate love to boring, stale love—from being madly in love to Maw and Paw at the Ranch. It's about as thrilling as rocking on the front porch together, watching the grass grow.

Many so-called experts say that as we age, our love mellows and becomes mature. We move past the passion of our early relationship and settle into a comfortable, stable, and secure love. I say, "Baloney!" I don't know about you, but I want my love to be more than mellow and comfortable. That doesn't sound like a whole lot of fun to me. I want my love with Sandy to be passionate. To be alive. To feel intense.

I'm not suggesting we can have passion 100 percent of the time. Frankly, no one has the stamina! What I am suggesting—no, I'm telling you—is that we can have passion on a regular basis. Passion is a part of every great relationship. If you have no passion in your marriage, you have nothing. Nothing! You don't really have a marriage at all. (I don't know what you call it, but it's not a marriage by God's definition.) You are only living together. Existing together is closer to the truth. You are business partners. Parents. Two persons tied together legally, but in no other way. Is this what you had in mind when you got married? I doubt it.

There's a better way. It's God's way. And it involves passion. Read the Song of Solomon, and you'll see God's idea of a real marriage. Solomon and the Shulammite woman were crazy about each other. Passion is splashed over every page of the book! God wouldn't make passion such a prominent part of this book if we all couldn't have it in our marriages, too. He wouldn't tease us like that! Every married couple can get and keep the same kind of passion that was percolating between Solomon and his wife.

That's exactly what God wants for you and your spouse. And I'm going to teach you how to achieve it. Actually, I pray that God will do the teaching. I'm just the messenger.

The Death of Passion

What happens to cause the death of passionate love? Why does this death happen to most of us four to ten years into our relationships? One main reason: We stop doing the things that create passionate love.

Our initial passion springs up without effort. When we first meet and are going out, the passion is just there! Boom! We instantly get it. It grabs us by the throat, and we are swept along by this amazing, powerful, intoxicating river. It's chemistry. It's infatuation. It's hormones. At least, in the beginning of a relationship. Our passion is not connected to the higher intellectual centers of the brain. For once, even the man's logic deserts him. It's all one big emotional chain reaction.

We have the feelings first. And the feelings motivate us to do things that are passionate, intense, and exciting. Feelings first, and then behavior. This is how all love relationships start. Because we are "in love," we become a couple. We date. We go out and do fun things together. We laugh and play and touch. Everything we do is driven by the feelings we have for each other.

As our original feelings peter out (hormones only carry us so far), we slowly stop doing loving behaviors. We end up, most of us, with the passion gone. Wondering what happened. Wondering why we are so far apart. We look at our spouse, and there's no spark. No heart-pumping, adrenaline-rushing reaction. There's just a certain fondness. An affection. A gosh-you're-a-nice-person familiarity. It's fine to feel that way about great-uncle Harvey or a household pet. But not about the person we married!

Right here, many couples quit. When their passion is gone, they think it's gone forever, and they'll never get it back. So, they throw in the marital towel. "It was a nice run, but this is the end of the road." The relationship is, for all intents and purposes, over. A slow, hideous death begins. The couple will do one of two things. They'll stay together out of duty and just bump along in a cold, passionless marriage. Or, they'll get divorced and try again with a new partner, and often the same cycle takes place.

American culture's answer to this loss of passion is divorce. Culture says: "Look, nobody stays together forever. Life is too short to keep on suffering in this marriage. You have only seventy or eighty years to live. Get out while you're still young enough to attract someone else. The kids will be fine. You're just hurting the kids anyway by staying in your marriage."

Millions of persons, non-Christians and Christians, are taking culture's advice. I should say Satan's advice. That's who is really sending this message.

It's too bad, because those who leave marriage when the passion leaves never get to the good stuff. They quit too soon! Real, deep, and intimate love is only reached after your initial passion runs out, after the "cloud nine" experience. That's when you can build the marriage God wants you to have.

And by the way, divorce always hurts the kids and goes on hurting. Divorce is, without question, the most devastating and traumatic event for children. Life goes on, and the children will recover. But don't fool yourself. Damage is done.

I see clients all the time in my office who want to divorce. They feed me culture's advice and try to persuade me to believe it. They are disappointed when they tell me: "We just fell out of love," and I reply: "I know. I believe you. Of course you did. Everybody does. That's not a good enough reason to divorce." Frustrated, they try again: "But, you don't understand. I don't love (fill in the blank with spouse's name) anymore." I respond: "I do understand. So? I'm not surprised. One partner always runs out of infatuation before the other. It just happened to be you. That's still no reason to get divorced."

I tell these clients that every couple loses their original love. It is a very difficult and painful place to be. But it is not unusual. It is universal. Then I tell them that now is the best time to build a real marriage. A marriage based not on infatuation, but on authentic love. The genuine article.

I tell them: "You haven't had a marriage yet. You've had a nice run of infatuation and hormones. That's over now. Good. You have a choice. You can divorce and have three, maybe four more infatuations before you die. And never know true love. Or, you can build one great love relationship with the person you're married to now. What's it going to be?"

I share God's perspective with these out-of-love clients: "God wants you to stay in your marriage. He wants you to avoid the pain and suffering divorce always inflicts on its victims. God's perspective is eternal. It's not eighty years, and it's all over. It's eighty years on earth, and then living forever in heaven or hell." I try to convince these clients that, with God's help, they can forge a brand-new marriage. Some have already been divorced and are still searching for love. I tell them they can find an intimate, forever love with their present marriage partner.

I'll tell you what I tell them: "Your marriage is dead. Go ahead and bury it. Let's start over and make a marriage that is filled with passion and life and love."

GETTING YOUR FEELINGS BACK

At the point in the marriage when you lose your passion, you have to do something revolutionary. Something you have never done before. You have to reverse the process. You have to begin doing loving behaviors in order to bring back the passion. You won't just wake up one morning and suddenly have the passion back. It doesn't work that way.

From now on, it will be behavior first, and then feelings. For the rest of your life as a couple, you will have to work hard at creating and maintaining passion. It's worth the effort, believe me, because the alternative is grim. Living without passion is depressing and draining and empty. And not glorifying or pleasing to God. This is not what God had in mind when He designed marriage.

God wants you to experience the deepest human love possible with your partner. That's what marriage is all about! And if you do the right things, you'll get a passionate love with your marriage partner. This love will be much deeper and much more fulfilling than the hormone-driven passion you had back at the beginning.

Passion is like a fire. You must keep adding logs to keep it going. Let's look at some logs that will put some life, some pizzazz, and some heat in your love.

EIGHTEEN

LOVE IS A FEELING

"Love is not a feeling. Love is a choice. It is an act of the will." If I hear this message one more time, I'll scream! It's been overplayed. Overused. Overdone. And I'm over it.

I hear these words, and so do you, from many well-meaning persons—pastors, authors, radio talk show hosts, theologians, Bible teachers, and even Christian psychologists.

I understand why they say it. There are a lot of divorces taking place based on feelings. One spouse doesn't "feel" in love anymore and so ends the marriage. These Christian leaders and commentators are trying to fight this wave of feelings-driven divorces. That's why they say, usually in solemn tones:

"You can't rely on your feelings. Feelings come and go. Love has nothing to do with feelings. It is simply a choice. You can choose to stay in the marriage. You can choose to do the right thing."

I agree! I want couples to stay married. I spend a good part of every week trying to convince couples to make the choice to stay in a conflicted marriage. There are certainly times when you can't rely on your feelings and must, by force of will, choose to do the right thing. These times of gutting out the pain and choosing to love do happen in every marriage. But they should not characterize your marriage. You shouldn't be gritting your teeth in order to force yourself to stay, every single day of every single month of every single year.

I know there are persons who are not able to feel love in their marriages. They are married to partners who don't even like them. Who refuse to communicate. Who refuse to love them the way they need to be loved. These persons must rely on love being a choice. That's all they have. With God's help, they can choose to stay. I have some good friends in this miserable situation. They're choosing to stay and have my utmost respect for that difficult, daily choice.

What I'm saying is that this scenario isn't God's Plan A. It is not what He wants for your marriage. He has not designed love to be only an intellectual act of the will.

Love is, in part, a choice. Sure it is. But that's not all it is. I'm afraid this "Love is a Choice" message has defined love as nothing more than a responsible series of choices. Love is a whole lot more than that.

There has been a backlash against feelings. Feelings have been cheapened and described as frivolous. Love as choice and behavior and act of will is being portrayed as much better than feelings. Feelings are being discounted and treated as unnecessary.

Listening to some of these Christian "experts," I get the distinct impression they don't like feelings. They're not comfortable with feelings. Feelings are bad. Nasty. Unreliable. Feelings just get you in trouble. They'd like feelings to just go away.

Well, I beg to differ. I'm coming to the defense of feelings. Feelings are just as important as choice in the arena of love. Not more important. But just as important.

Love is a choice. Love is also a feeling. A glorious, life-giving, supercharged, magnificent feeling.

If you don't have the feeling of love in your marriage, something's wrong. You need to choose to hang in there with your spouse if you don't have it. But if you do the right things, you'll get the feeling back. In fact, the feeling will be better than it ever was before. This isn't just me talking about feelings. I didn't make all this up in my head. It's God talking. God makes it clear in the Bible that love is a feeling.

SOLOMON AND HIS SWEETIE

You cannot read the Song of Solomon without getting hit in the face with the message: Love is a Feeling! The whole book is one big, whopping, pulsating feeling! Go ahead, read it. You'll see. Solomon and the Shulammite woman were crazy in love! Absolutely wild with passion about each other. And God loved every minute of it.

God gave Solomon and his woman their passionate love. He encouraged it. He blessed it. He was with the lovers on their wedding night when they consummated their marriage. He urged them to enjoy their first sexual intercourse (Song of Solomon 5:1, NAS).

You want a good description of marital love? Try this one, from Song of Solomon 8:6–7 (NAS):

> "Put me like a seal over your heart,
> Like a seal on your arm.
> For love is as strong as death,
> Jealousy is as severe as Sheol;
> Its flashes are flashes of fire,
> The very flame of the LORD.
> Many waters cannot quench love,
> Nor will rivers overflow it;
> If a man were to give all the riches of his
>   house for love,
> It would be utterly despised."

Whoa! This doesn't sound like just an act of the will to me. Love is like a blazing fire! Now, that's passion!

Passion was the driving force and main characteristic of this couple's relationship. Their passion remained strong and vibrant throughout the three phases of their life together: their courtship, their wedding, and the maturation of their marriage. In fact, their love and passion for each other improved and deepened over the years of their marriage (Song of Solomon 7:1–10, 8:13–14, NAS). One of the key reasons Solomon and the Shulammite didn't lose their passion was because they kept doing the loving behaviors they had done in their courtship days.

If God had wanted to teach us that passion ends and marital love inevitably becomes stale, He would have illustrated that with Solomon and the Shulammite. Their relationship would have grown cold, and they would have had to just keep choosing to stay together. But God didn't do that. He did just the opposite. In this book, God shows us in great detail His model of marriage. His model is two persons staying passionately in love throughout their entire relationship.

Song of Solomon teaches that love is a balance between behavior and feelings. Solomon and the Shulammite maintained their passionate feelings because they continued to do the right loving behaviors. You don't just choose to love. You need to choose to do the right behaviors, and that will produce the right feelings. The good, passionate feelings.

I want a Solomon-Shulammite woman marriage, don't you? I want all the feelings that go with love. I have these feelings with Sandy most of the time. Why? Because we communicate, and because we do romantic behaviors. I've already covered communication. It's time to look at romance.

YOU MUST BE ROMANTIC

Notice I said *must*. Romance is not an option if you want passion. Where there is romance, there is passion. You show me a couple without romance, and I'll show you a couple with a dying love.

Most of the couples I see in therapy have very little love left when they come in. One reason for this sad state of affairs is no romance is happening. Usually, no romance has happened for a long while. Typically when I ask couples when they last engaged in some kind of romantic behavior, I'm met with uncomfortable silence. "Well, Dr. Clarke. . . we, uh. . . Let's see, it was. . . No, no, I guess not. I really can't remember."

I ask them how they met, about the early days of their

relationship. Their eyes light up. There's a spark as they recall how they used to romance each other. They look back wistfully at how much fun they had during their courtship. Then I tell them one of the ways to breathe life into a dying love is through romance. With only a few exceptions, I recommend the restarting of romance right away.

Most of these couples look at me like I'm crazy. "What, take her out? I'd rather go out with a great white shark!" Or: "Be romantic with him? You've got to be kidding! He's about as romantic as a piece of lawn furniture."

These couples need romance. You and your spouse need romance. Romance is the beginning of passion. It creates the mood for passion.

CREATE THE "MOOD"

The mood is a warm, soft glow that opens your heart and your mouth to your partner. Solomon and the Shulammite woman were masters at creating the mood. It worked to give them passion. It'll work for you, too.

First, the mood opens your heart, and there's an openness, a vulnerability that wasn't present before. The wall comes down. (There's always a wall between a man and a woman. That wall must come down if intimacy is to happen.) Then, the mood opens your mouth, and you can say deep, meaningful, loving things. Not sweet nothings like:

"My special poopsie."

"My little peppermint patty."

"Mommy loves her big daddy."

But things like:

"I love you so much, honey."

"I'm glad God gave you to me."

"You are like a gazelle or a young stag."

   (Sorry, that was the Shulammite)

"You mean more to me than anyone else in the world."

Here's an emotion. Here's a reaction. Here's something personal. You'll both say personal things with the mood that you won't say without it. The mood always determines the level of conversation. Always. Think about it. You're having dinner in the middle of a family-style restaurant. Why, I don't know, but there the two of you are, surrounded by people. It's noisy. Bright lights. Kids are yelling.

What are the chances you'll create the mood there? Zero. Never in a million years. I've studied this. I've sent couple after couple into one of these restaurants and watched behind two-way mirrors and listened with hidden microphones. Nothing but superficial chatter!

Now, how about dinner in a small Italian place? A private corner. Quiet. Candlelight. An Italian guy named Luigi playing violin. Now, we're talking! Literally. What are the chances you'll get the mood here and talk on a deeper level? Very good!

In the early days of a relationship, this romantic mood is just there. It's always with you. It's automatic. You have it in the laundromat. You have it in the discount store parking lot. But after you've been together for a few years, this mood is just not there. It does not spontaneously come up.

Let me illustrate: I arrive home in the evening and step in the door to total chaos. Three girls are shrieking, crying, laughing hysterically. William, my three year old, runs over and grabs my leg. The floor is a minefield of toys and clothes. I look into the kitchen and see Sandy, who is making dinner. At least, I hope she's making dinner. Our eyes meet, and the world comes to a stop; she smiles softly, and we melt into each other's arms. . . .

Is this what happens? Of course not! The first part of the evening is focused on our kids. Homework, dinner, playtime. Later on, we create the mood ourselves after we put the kids to bed. At least, they're in their rooms. By the way, the kids don't have to be asleep before Sandy and I begin our moodmaking. I just want them away from us.

The kids will whine: "I can't go to sleep." "I'm not tired." My response: "I don't care. Stay awake all night if you want. Just don't bother me." Works like a charm.

Right after the kids are in their rooms, Sandy and I get on the couch and begin our twenty- to thirty-minute talk time. We create the mood because we've learned that when we have the mood, our conversations are better. We talk more openly and personally and intimately. And that's what we want.

If that's what you want, turn the page. I'm going to describe a number of carefully researched, time-tested ways to create a romantic mood.

NINETEEN

IT'S THE ROMANCE

What I'm about to say may cause some of you to question my manhood. It's an admission only a virile, confident man could make.

Well, here goes. I loved the old *Hart to Hart* television series. Remember that one? It's probably still playing on cable somewhere. It remains, in my opinion, the most romantic show in television history. It starred Robert Wagner and Stefanie Powers as a rich, beautiful, married couple who solved crimes in their spare time. These two were real jet-setters. They wore the finest clothes, drove the finest cars (actually, Max the chauffeur drove), and ate at the finest restaurants.

But the one thing that held my attention was the quality of their relationship. These two persons, at least on television, were deeply in love. They were incredibly, almost unbelievably, romantic.

On every single show, the romance between the Harts was the main theme. They surprised each other with cards and gifts. They dined by candlelight. They touched each other frequently (and tastefully). They must have kissed, at the bare minimum, forty times on each episode. They verbally expressed their love all the time. There were many *I love yous*. They were always saying gooey, sentimental things to each other.

For a couple who had been married awhile, they acted like a couple of kids. They were spontaneous and playful. Silly, even. They'd make jokes, tease in an affectionate way, and pull little pranks on each other. There was a lot of laughter. They always had fun together.

It was sappy. Mushy. Overkill sweet and syrupy. Kind of like an hour-long greeting card commercial. And I loved it. And it's just what you and I need in our marriages.

I want the kind of romance in my marriage that the Harts had. Yes, I do. King Solomon would have loved this show. He would have turned to the Shulammite woman during a commercial break and said: "Sweetheart, this American couple is just like us." Then, he would have kissed her and said some romantic thing to her.

If you think romance is silly and immature and unnecessary, fine. Get used to a cold, boring, and passion-free marriage. Personally, I want a full-strength marriage. I want to taste and enjoy every last ounce of passion with Sandy. Romance will get me there. Romance will get you there.

Here now is the Dave and Sandy Clarke guide to

romance. Think of it as the *Clarke to Clarke* romantic guide. These nine behaviors are guaranteed to stir up a little romance even in the crustiest, most lifeless marriage.

ONE DATE A WEEK

I'm a big believer in going out once a week on a date. This gets you away from the ranch. It's exciting. It's fun. (If you have kids, it gets you away from them!) You're dating—still courting each other! Your courtship should never end. The wedding usually kills the courtship. Don't let that happen to you!

Plan your dates. Be creative. When you get in the car, don't say to each other: "Well, what do you want to do tonight? Oh, I don't know, what do you want to do?" Going back and forth like this is pathetic! Don't be driving down the road deciding where you're going to eat. "Oh, there's a pancake house!"

Do what Sandy and I do. We take turns. This Saturday, I plan the date. I try not to plan something Sandy would hate, but it's my responsibility to come up with the idea. Next Saturday, she plans the date. And so on. Of course, you need to be romantic on the other days of the week. But this idea guarantees you'll be romantic at least once a week.

I can already hear your excuses. "We're too busy. We can't find a baby-sitter. We always go out with the kids. We can't afford it." Baloney. Baloney. Baloney. Baloney. Do you want to be romantic or don't you? It isn't easy to go out once a week, but it's worth it.

Hold Hands

When you're walking together, hold hands. That's what sweethearts do! I can't believe the number of couples I see walking along with no contact! Their hands are just swinging free. No! Not a good idea. What do you think your hands are for? God didn't give us waffle irons at the end of our arms. Two hands fit together real nice. So, hold hands!

I have a big picture window in the back of my office. I can see my clients walking in from the parking area and walking back out. I have special film on the window so I can see them, but they can't see me. Sneaky, huh? (Actually, it is to block the Florida sun.) I tell couples before they leave my office to hold hands on the way to their car. I tell them: "I'll be watching, and I'll rap on my window if you're not doing it." They laugh nervously and I say: "I'm serious."

My friends, I've seen miracles happen through my big window. I've seen marriages begin to change in the thirty feet from my back door to the parking lot. Just because couples held hands for the first time in who knows how long.

I saw an older couple, in their sixties, some time ago. They had a terrible marriage filled with resentment and bitterness. At the end of the session, I told them to hold hands on the way to the parking lot. They looked at me like I was crazy, but they did it.

I'm telling you, it was incredible. They held hands strolling down my walkway. It was the first time in forty years their hands had touched. As I watched, these two began to enjoy it. They had a bounce in their steps.

When they reached their car, the man turned and gave me a thumbs-up sign. Then, he threw the lady back for a kiss! Unfortunately, he lost his balance and her head hit the bumper.

Just kidding about the bumper part. But the rest of the story is true. This couple had much more work to do in therapy, but holding hands started them on the way to healing.

When I cover this topic in my marriage seminars, I tell the audience: "I'll be watching when this session is over. As you walk out of here, I'd better see some handholding! Do you hear me?" Many couples will hold hands, and I can see from their smiles and body language that a romantic feeling has been created.

WALK TOGETHER OUTSIDE

There's something about walking together (holding hands, of course) in a natural setting. It gives you a nice, easygoing, and romantic feeling of closeness.

Take the beach, for example. What is it about water? Water is beautiful, soothing, and pretty romantic. Take off your shoes and socks. You always walk on the beach in your bare feet. (Unless it's winter and you'd get frostbite.) You walk along with the water lapping on the shore. You feel the soft sand crunching under your feet. The big, beautiful sky is open before you. The sun slowly sets on the horizon. Now, you tell me. Is this romantic, or what?

If you hate the beach or don't live near a beach, any natural setting will do—a park, a lake, a river, a wooded area. Even walking in your neighborhood can be romantic. As long as you're alone and holding hands.

Slow Dance to Music

Put some romantic music on the stereo or CD player. You could play beautiful, soft instrumental pieces. Or, some of your favorite love songs. Sandy and I like the Carpenters and Barry Manilow. (That's right, Barry Manilow.) Music is powerful. It can touch us and move us. We use music to worship, to open up our hearts to God. We can use music to create romance, to open up our hearts to each other.

With the lights down low, just hold each other close and slowly sway to the music. You don't need dancing lessons. If you're going to dance in public, get lessons. But in the privacy of your own home, no one's watching. If you're having trouble talking on a deeper level, try slow dancing before you talk. It's amazing how it can open you up!

Some of you are thinking: "Oh, Dave, really! I'd be too embarrassed to dance." I say: "Loosen up! Let yourselves go a little bit!" Try thinking of it as hugging to music! Sway, rock, take a spin around the room. If you're not quite ready to dance, at least sit on the couch and hold hands as you listen to the music. It's a start.

Watch Romantic Movies

This is a real winner. Sit down, just the two of you, and watch a romantic movie. You can catch one on television or rent one.

Sandy and I like the old classics. They're clean and well made. *Casablanca. To Have and Have Not. North by Northwest. Holiday Inn.* And the old screen couples are great! The romantic sparks really fly. Spencer Tracey and Katherine Hepburn. Humphrey Bogart and Lauren Bacall. Cary Grant and Audrey Hepburn.

Sit *together* on the love seat or couch. Not one of you in a chair and one on the couch. Not both in chairs. Come on! Being four or five feet apart defeats the whole purpose! You are close so you can touch. Kiss. Make out. As you watch the movie, the romantic interplay on the screen transfers to the two of you and your relationship. It's not Humphrey Bogart falling in love with Lauren Bacall. It's Bob falling in love with Betty!

The men are thinking: "Oh, no. These are chick flicks!" That's right. They are. Guess who you're married to? A chick! Go ahead, men, watch these movies. No other men will know. You won't regret it, believe me.

CANDLELIGHT DINNERS AT HOME

Nice, out-of-the-way restaurants are a good idea, but you can recreate the same atmosphere in your own home. Put the kids to bed early. Use a nice tablecloth. Get out the candles. Pick up some food from a decent restaurant and bring it home.

Use classy, romantic glasses. Don't bring out your old, stained plastic glasses! Did Cary Grant and Eva Marie Saint use paper cups on the famous train scene in *North by Northwest*? No!

And use the good china, will you? What is it about china? It's another woman thing! China is passed down for generations and never used! We must take care of the china. We can't touch it. We must pass it along intact to the next generation, so they can have it and not use it. Look, your great-grandma won't be upset if you break the china. She's dead!

You have a candlelight dinner every month or every couple of months, and you see what happens. It's classy. It's romantic. It creates the mood. It'll help you talk more deeply and touch more intimately.

WRITE CARDS AND LETTERS

Writing is a lost art. It can be very romantic. You need to make it a part of your relationship.

Sandy and I were separated the entire year before our wedding. Talk about a tough engagement. I wouldn't recommend it. What kept us close was letters—we wrote a lot of letters during that year. Each of us wrote three or four letters a week. Love letters! I couldn't wait to read one of Sandy's letters. The absolute highlight of my day was finding a letter from my sweetheart in my seminary dorm mailbox.

Very few couples write cards and letters to each other. If they wrote before getting married, they dropped the practice right after the wedding. "We're living together now. We don't have to write anymore. Right?"

Wrong. Keep writing each other, and you'll keep your romance and love alive. God wrote us a love letter. It's called the Bible. If God thought it was a good idea, it must be a good idea.

Go out, each of you, and buy a stack of romantic cards at the card shop or a Christian bookstore. Then, give one to your partner every few weeks. Leave the card on your sweetheart's pillow. Put it by your lover's place at the dining room table. Send the card in the mail. Everybody loves to get personal mail.

My dad, Bill Clarke, has sent my mom, Kathy, cards in the mail for years. He goes to great lengths to surprise her. (If you knew my mom, you'd know that's pretty tough to do.

She doesn't miss much.) Dad will use all different kinds of type and handwriting on the envelope so Mom won't realize it's from him. He's even had other people address the letter so she won't recognize the handwriting. It's a beautiful romantic game for them, and it works.

By the way, men, always write loving words in a card. Do you notice all that blank space in a card? Do you know what that's for? Trees have died for that space. It's for your personal message to your wife! Don't just sign a card: "Love, Bob." This packs all the punch of a lead balloon. These two words aren't all that meaningful for your wife. She knows you didn't write the printed words in the card! She wants a personal, romantic note from your heart to her heart. You can tell her how much you love her. Compliment her physical beauty. Thank her for all she does for you. Mention the great time you had together on your date two nights ago. You get the idea.

Occasionally, about once every two months, write a one-page letter to your partner. This goes for men and women. I'm talking a full-fledged love letter here! When *was* the last time you gave your sweetheart a real, honest to goodness love letter? I thought so. Get to work! Don't type this, either. It's not a report.

A WEEKEND GETAWAY

I think it's a great idea to have a weekend together, alone, at least once a year. It's a romantic escape from life's stresses and routines. You get away from the kids. The job. The neighbors.

The anniversary is a neat time to use for this getaway. Your anniversary is a very special date, and you ought to make a huge deal out of it. Not just a card, a kiss on the cheek, and mumbling something like: "Thanks for the memories."

The two of you can go to a bed and breakfast. Or to a beach place. Or to a place in the mountains. Or to a beautiful hotel. Who cares? As long as you're together, it doesn't make much difference where you go. If the budget's tight, go to a cheaper place. If all else fails, farm your kids out and stay home together. The peace and quiet will deafen you. A home without children is a home of romance.

Wherever you end up, it is your love nest. A time to revitalize your relationship. A time to talk for hours at a stretch. A time to dream about the future. A time to touch and love each other without fear of interruption.

TELL YOUR PARTNER
WHAT IS ROMANTIC FOR YOU

Spend time, periodically, describing for each other romantic places and experiences. Brainstorm. Throw out to your partner scenarios you would find romantic. Don't keep these ideas a secret. That way, you'll never get your needs met.

When Sandy tells me what she finds romantic (a place at the beach, a certain restaurant, what she'd like to do during a date), what do I do? If you answered: "You jot it down on your pad so you won't forget," give yourself a gold star. I file her romantic fantasy and start to plan it. When we do it, what are my chances for a super-romantic time? Sky-high! Absolutely 100 percent!

Why? Because she's flattered and impressed I remembered. She feels loved because I took the time to plan her idea and surprise her with it. But the main reason is she told me what she considered romantic! Like a lot of men, I don't like to guess. I like to know that there's an ironclad guarantee I'm going to score points on the marriage scoreboard.

These are just nine romantic behaviors. I could go on and on. Use these. They work for Sandy and me. But don't stop with these nine. Get your minds in a romantic gear and come up with your own ideas.

Keep in mind that these romantic behaviors won't create passion right away. At first, it'll be awkward and uncomfortable, especially if you two are out of practice. But don't get discouraged. Keep on doing them. Eventually, you'll get the romantic mood. And if you get the mood, you'll get the passion.

TWENTY

TOUCHING, TALKING, AND TREMENDOUS SEX

To love passionately, you must have a healthy physical relationship. That's right. I'm going to talk about sex. I waited
until Chapter Twenty because so many important steps need
to happen before good sex can happen: communication, needs
met, the romance, and the emotional connection. I have a
message for all you men who picked up this book and began
reading here in Chapter Twenty. Go back and read the first
nineteen chapters because you're not ready yet.

Wouldn't you just know it? Men and women see physical touch very differently. Dear God, can't we be the same

in just this one area? Please? No, I'm afraid not. God knows best and, sexually speaking, He has put men on the North Pole and women on the South Pole.

MEN AND TOUCH

For men, touch is foreplay. Its only purpose is to lead to intercourse. I mean, isn't that the point? When a man touches his woman or she touches him, the theme from the movie *Rocky* starts playing in his head: bum ba da bum ba da bum ba da bum. . . . He immediately thinks of sex, intercourse, the whole nine yards. He wants complete sexual release.

When a man gets sexually excited (and it doesn't take much), he wants to orgasm in intercourse, and he wants to do it as soon as possible. A man doesn't mind touching if he knows the touching is going to lead to intercourse.

Every man hates to hear these words from his woman: "Let's just cuddle." No! Good grief, no! For a man, cuddling is like getting the bronze medal in the Olympics. It's better than nothing, but not nearly what he had in mind.

This male approach to sex sounds selfish and, in part, it is. But keep in mind, ladies, that we men naturally express our love for you physically. Touching you and entering you in intercourse is our way of saying: "I love you." Unfortunately, our somewhat crude approach ends up making you feel anything but loved and cherished.

WOMEN AND TOUCH

For women, touch means closeness. Feeling warm, cared for,

and secure. Go figure! Women see touch as a way to achieve emotional connection. They do not look past touch to intercourse. Touch is not the prelude; it is part of the whole act.

Intercourse for a woman, as touch begins, is down the road ten miles. She isn't thinking: "Hey, we're touching. I hope we can have intercourse in ten minutes!"

Listen to this, men. A woman will not, cannot, enjoy intercourse unless she first has an emotional connection to you. You can be the greatest lover in the world, and it will make no difference without this connection. She needs talk, interaction, and understanding before she can be open to you sexually. I don't like this any more than you do, but it's the way God made women.

When a woman knows a man is touching her only because he wants intercourse (which, frankly, is what happens most of the time), she feels cheap and insulted, her personhood and needs rejected. She can feel like a prostitute in her own house, with her own husband! Without the emotional connection, if she consents to intercourse, she is far from a warm and willing partner. She will resent sex or endure it as a duty.

These are harsh words, but true words. I talk to a lot of women in my therapy office in Tampa, and this is what they tell me. They're just punching a time clock in bed, unable to enjoy intercourse. And unable to experience the full measure of pleasure and release in sex with their husbands.

Now, there's no right or wrong here. Neither partner is deliberately trying to hurt the other. Men aren't just selfish animals who can't control themselves. Really. Women don't hold back sex because they enjoy seeing a grown man cry. Really. It's the incredibly different way we perceive touch!

She's Cold,
and He's Frustrated

For many couples, this big difference in how touch is perceived leads to serious problems in the physical relationship. The woman becomes cold and uninterested in sex. She flinches every time the man touches her. The man becomes very frustrated, confused, and resentful. He isn't sure what's wrong and doesn't know how to approach the woman.

Sex becomes increasingly awkward and mechanical. Intercourse becomes less and less frequent. When it does occur, it is nothing more than a brief biological act and not the joyful time of communication and release God designed. The man and woman stop touching each other in healthy spontaneous ways because it hurts too much.

This sexual gridlock can happen to many couples in their twenties, thirties, and forties! The truth is, you can have healthy, vibrant sex well into your seventies and eighties. Now, it may take longer at this age. It might take a week to complete intercourse! But you'll be retired. You'll have the time.

Touch for
Foreplay and Closeness

To get touch and regular intercourse back in your relationship, learn to use touch for both foreplay and closeness. Men are right: Touch is foreplay. It's a great way to prepare for intercourse. Women are right: Touch means closeness. It's a wonderful way to feel emotionally connected.

When there is touch, the man is automatically on the

physical level, and the woman is automatically on the emotional level. There's no changing this fact of sexual life. What needs to change initially is the man's behavior. As the God-ordained leader in the relationship, the man must bite the bullet and learn to be patient in the sexual process.

If the man can wait and not push for intercourse when touch occurs, he and the woman have a good chance to move through three critical stages. Good, healthy sex always includes these stages.

Stage One begins when touch begins. It is fairly brief and consists of gentle, no pressure, low-key touching by both partners. If the woman is not pressured to move quickly to more intense touching and intercourse, she will feel loved. Without pressure, she will relax.

It's nice to be with a relaxed woman and not one who is defensive and tight as a drum. This relaxed woman will be able to receive touch and give touch. And, listen to this, men: She will be much more likely to move to Stages Two and Three.

In Stage Two, the man and woman create an emotional connection. They join on the emotional level by touching and talking. Most men don't realize that you can touch and talk at the same time! Well, you can. And you need to, in order to meet the woman's need for emotional closeness.

Men, have you ever noticed that your woman likes to talk during touching? Drives you crazy, doesn't it? She talks because she finally has a captive audience. Because she loves you. Because she wants and needs to feel close to you.

But this Stage Two isn't just about the woman's need for emotional closeness. It's about the man's need for emotional closeness. Men, you have the same need! You just are not aware of it and usually blow right past it in your hormone-driven rush to intercourse. Men, if you can slow down and talk to the woman as you touch her some very good things happen. You feel closer to her. She feels closer to you. And you are both ready for Stage Three.

Stage Three is intercourse. (Thought we'd never get here, didn't you?) When the man and woman proceed to intercourse (twenty minutes later, two hours later, the next morning, the next evening), both are prepared to move successfully to the physical level. Both can now be open and vulnerable sexually.

In Stage Three, a man needs to continue to touch his wife in gentle, loving ways. A high percentage of women report they do not—are not able to—achieve orgasm during intercourse. Most women will reach orgasm only when the man takes the time to caress and pleasure her.

I believe these stages are God's design for the sexual life of a married couple. Both partners have to be patient as they move through the stages. The woman has to wait for the man to be emotional, to talk and connect in conversation. The man has to wait for the woman to be physical, to be ready to give herself to him freely and fully.

Sex is emotional. Sex is physical. Sex is also spiritual. God intends for sexual intercourse to be a complete coming together of a man and a woman in all three of these areas.

TALK ABOUT SEX

It's amazing how many couples never talk to each other about the physical part of their relationship. I mean, never! It's too awkward, too personal, too risky, too embarrassing. It's also impossible to develop healthy touch and intercourse if you don't talk about it. An excellent way to learn more—more about the whole act, more about each other—is to read a good book about sex together. It can open door after door.

Men and women, get into the habit of talking about sex at neutral times. By neutral, I mean not during your times of touching and sex. You're nowhere near the bed during these discussions. Don't be critical, or offer suggestions that might be interpreted as critical, in bed during sex.

Discuss the differences between men and women in the area of touch. Tell your partner what is blocking you from really relaxing and enjoying touch. Describe when you want and don't want to be touched. Describe in detail how you want to be touched. What do you like? What do you not like?

Tell the truth. "I would really enjoy it if we. . ." or, "I enjoy. . ." Whoa, this would be tough to hear but better late than never. Many persons could have a closet full of Oscars for all the times they've pretended to enjoy sex. And it's not always the woman who is not interested in sex and has to be coaxed into the bedroom. In about 20 to 25 percent of couples, the roles are reversed. The man resists sex, and the woman pursues him. He avoids physical intimacy, and the woman becomes frustrated and feels continually rejected.

There are always reasons for either partner feeling uncomfortable with sex. The only way out is dealing with the issue directly. The resisting partner must find the courage, with God's help, to talk openly and honestly with the spouse about what's going on inside.

All couples have sexual problems. That's right. I said *all* couples. The only difference is between couples who talk about their sexual problems and couples who do not. The couples who do not discuss sex will never have a deeply intimate, satisfying sex life. The couples who do talk about sex have a good chance—almost 100 percent—to develop and maintain a great sex life.

When you talk about your sexual problems, you can actually discover what is blocking you. You are also being vulnerable, and so automatically you reach a deeper level with your partner. With the truth on the table and the two of you connecting on a deeper level, you can work together to resolve your sexual problems. Together is the only way you can resolve them, since sex involves both of you.

Make sure you see any sexual problem as a joint problem, one you both have. It's not: "You've got a problem. Fix it and get back to me." It's not even: "I'll help you with your problem." It needs to be: "We have a problem. Let's work on it together."

Ninety percent of sexual difficulties can be fixed with open, frank dialogue between the man and woman. In some cases, the couple will need to see a psychologist or physician to address psychological/medical issues. Always go together because it's a shared problem. Even if professional help is needed, you still have to talk in order to work through the problem as a team.

If you don't talk about your physical relationship, nothing can change. Neither partner has any idea how to improve sex. If you talk about it, together you can make significant changes. Talk regularly, at least once a month, to keep up-to-date and stay on track.

In addition to talking about sex at neutral times, learn to cut specific deals in your sex life. Give up the idea that sex is natural and spontaneous. After the honeymoon, you can kiss that notion good-bye. Let's have a moment of silence for our honeymoon sex. Oh, those were the days! Sex was anytime, anyplace, and more than once a day. No preparation.

No stages. No obstacles. No problems. Okay, that's enough. Time to move on in the real world.

After the first year of marriage, sex is a whole new ball game. There is preparation. There are stages. There are obstacles. You both must overcome problems. Now, you have to work at it.

It is extremely rare that once touch begins both partners immediately want intercourse. What you do at this point is critically important. On the front side of touching, just as it begins in Stage One, tell each other what you want and why. It's the unspoken things that can kill us! The more specific you are with your needs and expectations, the less misunderstanding and hurt there will be.

Tell Him the Truth

Women, as touch begins, tell the man the truth. If you just want to touch without intercourse, say so. Tell him before he really gets his motor running. Do you know what it's like to tell a man you don't want intercourse ten minutes into touching? It's like stepping on the track in front of a drag racer who is going one hundred and eighty miles an hour and saying: "Stop, please." Ladies, that's not nice. It's not fair. It's cruel. And by the way, don't use the word "cuddle" in your explanation.

Women, tell the man why you're not ready for intercourse. The man will still be disappointed, but it helps to have an explanation. Don't use the age-old, general excuses: "I have a headache" (unless you really do), "I'm not in the mood," and "Oh, not now, honey." These don't tell the man anything.

Give him the real reason. It may be personal. Bad day, too stressed, self-esteem down, fatigue. Or it may have to do with the relationship. An unresolved conflict, anger at the man, hurt feelings. The man has a right to know, and you'll feel better getting it off your chest.

Finally, ladies, tell the man when you'd like to have intercourse. Give the poor guy some hope, something to look forward to. And don't say: "Well, let's see. . .how about two weeks from Tuesday?" Unless there are serious problems in the relationship, don't make him wait too long. God wants married couples to have sex on a regular basis. In 1 Corinthians 7:3–5, Paul gives only one reason sex is to be interrupted. That reason is for prayer over an issue that is heavy on their hearts.

Now, keep in mind that there is a lot of exciting, physical touching you can do short of intercourse. It's called making out. Petting. Do I have to paint you a picture? Remember back when you were dating? You probably went too far at times and felt guilty afterwards. The good news is, God has forgiven you for this. He's over it. You can do all that petting now, without the guilt! Since you're married, it's okay. Put simply, God wants you to do it.

Many couples have virtually no touch except during intercourse. That's not right! That's not healthy! Men, don't sulk off if you can't get intercourse. Women, don't go completely cold and pull back from all touch just because you're not prepared for intercourse. Make out! Pet! Go ahead!

When neither partner wants or needs orgasm, just discuss up front what level of touch you'll enjoy. You can kiss, caress, make out, and have a wonderful time. All without orgasm. All without intercourse.

There will be times when the two of you decide you

won't have intercourse. But, at least one partner wants orgasm. Guess what? One or both partners can still achieve orgasm, outside of intercourse. There's no law against it. It's called mutual nonintercourse orgasm. At least, that's what I call it. With clothes on or off, you go through as much foreplay as you want. Then, one at a time, you stimulate your partner to orgasm. If just one partner wants orgasm, fine. If both want orgasm, fine.

A very common scenario is the woman not wanting intercourse and the man really wanting orgasm. Most men have a biological need to release semen, to ejaculate, on a regular basis. Ladies, help us out. Of course, the roles could be reversed. It might be the man not wanting intercourse and the woman wanting orgasm. Either way, you have a responsibility to satisfy your partner.

Prepare the Woman

Men, you need to ask for intercourse in advance. Even before Stage One, if possible. Most women do not respond well to surprises.

Picture this scene. It's the end of the day, and the man is in bed. The woman is in the bathroom washing her face, brushing her teeth, and doing whatever else women do to get ready for bed. The man has said nothing about sex or much of anything else the whole day. As the woman leaves the bathroom and comes to the bed, the man pats her pillow and says: "This is your lucky night, sweetie." The woman smiles and says: "I was hoping you'd say that, big boy!" And then she jumps into bed. I don't think so. What really happens is she's horrified, stunned, taken by surprise.

She is completely unable to shift into sexual gear. Women aren't made that way.

Men, women need preparation. They need to be courted, loved, their emotional needs met before they're ready for intercourse. Unlike the hot babes on television and in the movies, real women cannot be sexual at the drop of a hat or a pair of pants.

Sexually speaking, men are light switches. Click, they're on. Women are the lights at baseball fields. I was with my kids one night in the stands waiting for my wife Sandy's softball game to start. Someone had forgotten to turn on the big field lights, and it was pitch dark. The umpire hit the switch, and we all watched as the lights slowly came on. It took fifteen to twenty minutes for the lights to slowly, slowly increase until they were fully illuminated. I stood up and said out loud to the crowd in the stands: "Hey, those lights are like a woman sexually!" No, I didn't. But I was thinking it. It takes a woman time to come on sexually.

Men, set a time in advance for intercourse and start getting your wife ready. If you want intercourse tonight, ask her as soon as possible. Ask her in the morning, at lunchtime, in the early evening. You need time to emotionally connect!

Call and ask if you can run any errands for her on your way home. When you get home, kiss her on the lips and say: "I love you." The very next words out of your mouth ought to be: "What can I do to help you tonight?" Then, do what she asks. Do chores, help with the kids, set the table, and whatever else she needs.

As soon as the kids are out of your hair, ask your wife to sit down with you and talk. Tell her about your day. Ask what's going on in her life and listen, really listen, to her. Pray together for family concerns, friends, and your relationship.

When you follow this pattern, you've prepared your wife emotionally for a time of physical intimacy.

You'll get a wife who feels loved by you. You'll get more making out and nonintercourse touching than you do now. You'll get more intercourse than you do now, and the love-making will be much more passionate and exciting. You wife will desire you, because she'll be emotionally connected to you.

TWENTY-ONE

LET'S SEE SOME REAL PASSION!

Intercourse is an important part of a marriage. God says so. Intercourse is a beautiful picture of marital intimacy. All three areas of the relationship—physical, emotional, and spiritual—come together in a powerful way in the act of intercourse.

God, in the Song of Solomon, goes to great lengths to describe the wonder, majesty, and pleasure of intercourse. In 1 Corinthians 7:1–5, the Lord clearly teaches that intercourse is to be a healthy, regular practice between husband and wife.

In the physical area of marriage, intercourse gets all of the attention. Intercourse is the Great Big Grand Pooh-bah. The Big Cheese. The Main Attraction. It's what everybody wants to talk about—American society is obsessed with intercourse. There are literally hundreds of books, video-tapes, and seminars available to help you and your partner improve your intercourse. The central message of all these "helpful" programs is: If you want great passion, you've got to have great intercourse.

Look, I'm not saying intercourse isn't important. It is. I want you to enjoy it. But it's a little overrated. It's getting too big for its own britches. It is not the only game in town. In fact, intercourse is not the main source of physical passion in a marriage. It's great, but it's not Number One. Do you know what is the Number One source of physical passion in a marriage? Basic physical affection.

Doesn't sound too exciting, does it? Well, it is. It's these nonintercourse, daily touches that make up the bulk of a couple's physical relationship. When you learn how to use this type of touching in the right ways, your level of passion will go off the charts.

If you're depending on intercourse alone to fill your passion tank, you're in trouble. You simply don't have intercourse often enough. You don't have intercourse every day, do you? That's impossible. Well, not impossible, but highly unlikely.

FOREPLAY FOR FOREPLAY'S SAKE

One of the keys to developing real passion in a marriage is the skillful and frequent use of basic physical affection. I'm not talking about a pat on the back or a hand on the shoulder. I'm talking about sexual activity. What I'm about to describe will get your motor going. It will feel great. It will be intense.

It is not intercourse, however. It may lead to intercourse, but that's not the real point. It is foreplay for foreplay's sake. It is a kind of sexual affection that stands alone. Strictly by itself, it meets needs that intercourse cannot meet.

This special brand of daily foreplay will do wonders for your relationship. It creates passion. It connects you. It communicates love. It feels good. It reduces stress. It is great preparation for intercourse, whether you end up having it or not. It can even serve a critical role in preparing the two of you for talk. Nonintercourse foreplay can be particularly effective in helping the man open up in verbal communication. As long as he understands up front that intercourse is off the table, this type of touching can really motivate him to talk more personally.

I can hear some of you. "Oh, Dave, you don't understand. I'm just not an affectionate person. I'm not a toucher. I never have been." It may be true that you never have been, but that can change. It needs to change if you want passion and all these other benefits.

Listen to me, you naturally unaffectionate persons. GET OVER IT. If you weren't married, it wouldn't make any difference. But you are married, and your partner needs you to be involved in touch and affection and foreplay. I'm not asking you to do this for any other person. Just your spouse. It'll be hard, but you can change.

God didn't give us all this skin for nothing! It's supposed to be touched. Often. And thoroughly enjoyed. And, most of the time, touching will be done outside of intercourse.

Here are some practical how-to principles in the three areas of foreplay for foreplay's sake.

REAL KISSING

You know what I mean. Long, involved, somewhat wet, heartfelt smackers. Sucky face! I'm talking about open-mouth kissing. Kissing with a punch!

Stop giving each other those pathetic little pecks! "See you tonight". . .peck. "Have a nice day, honey". . . peck. "Welcome home". . .peck. Two sets of bone-dry lips touching for a millisecond. The peck is so fast the human eye can barely pick it up. Why do you even bother? You might as well shake hands.

The poofy-lip kiss is another miserable excuse for a kiss. Here, the lips are bunched together and shoved out an inch or more from the mouth. It's as if the kisser wants to keep the "kissee" as far away as possible. My research shows this is the kind of kiss eighty-year-old great-grandmothers give their great-grandchildren.

We also have the sound-effect kiss. In this ludicrous scenario, the kisser doesn't even deign to touch the lips of the spouse. The kisser just makes the sound of a kiss and walks off! This one's a real mystery to me. Why would you make a kissing sound when the person is right there with you? Why not just kiss the person?

These three kisses have absolutely no place in a marriage. Why, they are not kisses at all! You might as well be kissing the wall. It's about as exciting. Are you kissing your Aunt Sarah? No! You're kissing your beloved marriage partner. Your lover! Your soul mate. Your precious sweetheart.

To give anything less than your best, top quality kisses is an insult to your spouse and your marriage. It's an outrage! It needs to stop!

Do you think Solomon and the Shulammite pecked each other? Do you think they kissed with poofy lips? Do you really think they did the sound-effect kiss? No way! These two married sweethearts lived thousands of years ago, but baby, they knew how to kiss!

The second verse in the Song of Solomon, the very second verse in the book, is a kissing verse.

> *"May he kiss me with the kisses of his mouth!*
> *For your love is better than wine."* (1:2, NAS)

I draw a number of conclusions from this verse. First, God must think kissing is pretty important! Second, the Shulammite was talking about kisses—plural. This lady wanted multiple kisses! Third, there's an exclamation point at the end of the first phrase. The woman was obviously talking about real kisses. Ground-shaking, teeth-rattling kisses!

It's no surprise to me that God's book on physical love in marriage begins with kissing. Very often, kissing starts off the whole chain of physical affection.

If you can't kiss properly, you can't do anything else! You aren't going anywhere else in the physical area. You're stopped at the door and can't fully explore the wonderful pleasures God has for you in physical intimacy.

Song of Solomon 4:11 (NAS) is probably the greatest, most explicit verse in the Bible about kissing:

> *"Your lips, my bride, drip honey;*
> *Honey and milk are under your tongue."*

Most of the Bible commentators I checked think honey and milk in this verse refer to the richness of the land of Canaan. No, it doesn't! Honey and milk as used here have nothing to do with the land of Canaan! No doubt these commentators don't know how to kiss, either. Real kissing tastes good! That's what the verse is saying. Solomon connects honey and milk to his bride's tongue, not Canaan. If this isn't a reference to French kissing, I don't know what is.

When was the last time you were decently kissed by your spouse? I'll bet it's been a while. You two know how to kiss each other. You used to do it all the time. It's time to get back to that kind of kissing. You can start right away. Before you go your separate ways in the morning, lay a real gum-scorcher of a kiss on your partner. Not a half an hour long. You don't grab each other and throw yourselves to the floor. But you plant a smooch you'll both remember. And when you see each other after a long day, it's time for another great kiss. Did you miss each other? Are you happy to see each other again? If so, show it!

There ought to be some serious kissing every day. In the evenings, when the kids are in their rooms, hit the couch and do some making out. You ought to be talking and kissing. Start giving out some Song of Solomon 4:11 kisses and you'll have your old, almost forgotten friend Passion right there on the couch with you.

REAL HUGGING

There's nothing like a good, full-body hug. All the right parts touching. It's intimate. It's sexual. It's supposed to be! Not with your Aunt Sarah. Of course not. But with your lover? You better believe it.

My research with hundreds of couples, both in therapy and in my seminars, has revealed three main mistakes in hugging.

The first mistake is being a stick. When you try to hug a stick, he remains ramrod straight. He's as stiff as a board. His hands are held rigidly at his sides. He just takes the hug with no response. He acts as if he's taking a dose of castor oil or some other foul-tasting medicine.

The second mistake is being a V-shaped hugger. Many women are guilty of this particular mistake. This type of hugger stands at a distance and gingerly leans forward with her chest extended. With her chest barely grazing the chest of the hugger and her backside pushed out, she forms a V. She briefly touches the other person's shoulders and then releases them and steps away.

The final mistake is the side hugger. Here, the hugger sneaks up to the side of the person. I say sneaks because this hugger moves quickly to avoid any chance of a head-on hug. Once in position at the side, he or she puts an arm carefully around the shoulders of the "huggee" and pulls gently. The sides of the two bodies touch briefly, and then it's over.

All these mistakes are efforts to avoid the full intimacy of a face-to-face hug. If you're hugging your Aunt Sarah, any of these three hugs are appropriate. But when it's your spouse, the only hug you should even consider is the total body contact, wraparound hug. Face-to-face. Every significant body part touching. Arms wrapped around each other. Firm pressure.

And it must be a lingering hug. You act as if you're enjoying it and don't want to stop. Twenty to thirty seconds long is about right. You might even kiss afterwards. It'd be a shame to miss the opportunity.

REAL PLEASURING

Pleasuring is a lost art in most marriages. Early in their marriages, most couples do a lot of mutual pleasuring. You know, nonintercourse touching. Heavy petting. Massaging. Caressing. It was fun, wasn't it? Exciting and invigorating. Very sensual. But after a few years of marriage, you quit pleasuring, didn't you? If you touch now, it's only for a brief period of foreplay before intercourse.

I talked about pleasuring in Chapter Twenty, so I won't cover the same ground. The point I want to make here is that pleasuring is usually a key to helping a man open up in communication. Most men I talk to have one particular area of their body that, when stimulated by the woman, motivates them to talk more freely. No, ladies, it's not the part you're thinking. It is a nongenital part. And it's nothing weird or kinky.

Here are some of the conversation-triggering body parts men have told me about: hair, scalp, neck, back, face, earlobes (I'm serious), chest, legs, buttocks, fingers, calves, upper arms, and feet.

These men have told me that when their particular "erogenous" zone is massaged by their woman, it gives them great pleasure. It also makes them feel loved and cherished by her. And close to her. And when they feel close to her, they are more likely to share personally. Sound crazy, ladies? It's not. It really works. Give it a try. Ask your husband what his area is. If he's not sure, start experimenting. You'll find it.

Men, keep in mind that the real point of this physical

stimulation is conversation. Sure, you will be sexually aroused. But do not push for intercourse. Allow yourself to open up and talk to the woman. Sometimes, you'll both agree up front, before the touching, that you will move to intercourse. Fine. But, before intercourse, you still need to talk with her.

Other times, you'll both agree that intercourse won't happen. In those cases, the stimulation of your special area will produce nonintercourse, physical pleasure and verbal communication. And that's all. But that's enough!

When Sandy rubs my feet, I'm putty in her hands. It sends me into orbit. My brain waves change. I feel closer to her, and it puts me in the mood for conversation. It's too bad for Sandy my area is my feet, but that's life.

This pleasuring of a specific body part works for the ladies, too. If you live with a female clam, men, then you need to try this technique on her. If your woman isn't a clam, you still need to pleasure her. It won't be for the purpose of getting her to talk. She's already talking. But it will still feel good to her and help meet her nonintercourse intimacy needs.

Work Together for Passion

You ought to be touching in meaningful, passionate ways every day. In the morning. In the evening. Whenever you are together. Of course, if you have kids, you wait until you are alone to move into the more intimate, nonintercourse touching.

Touching and pleasuring will be difficult because you two are so different.

Men are usually more into touching and sexual activity.

It's much more natural for men. Men think about touching constantly. Men, you want to touch every day, don't you? Women have to learn how to touch.

Women usually are more into talking and emotional connection. It's as natural as breathing for women. Women think about talking and emotionally connecting constantly. Women, you want to talk every day, don't you? Men have to learn how to talk.

Men and women, you have to work together to create passion every day. Or, at least, three or four times a week. But to get passion three or four times a week, you have to be trying every day. Just like conversations, you'll hit a certain percentage of passionate times if you deal in volume.

Create the mood with romance. Work through the stages, touching and talking. Sometimes you'll move on to intercourse, sometimes you won't. But either way, you'll move on to passion. If you work together and practice this kind of touching and talking, you know what's going to happen? You'll get passion back into your relationship. And if you keep these behaviors going, you'll never lose your passion.

TWENTY-TWO

THE SECRET TO GENUINE INTIMACY

I'm sure you know persons who have been divorced. Have you ever wondered why so many marriages are ending in divorce? No one seems immune from the divorce epidemic. Movie stars. Famous athletes. The rich. The middle class. The poor. Persons who know Jesus Christ and go to church. Atheists. Family members. Friends. Coworkers. Neighbors.

Many of you reading these words have gone through the pain of divorce. Looking back, do you know what went wrong? You just couldn't seem to make the relationship work, could you? You just didn't have any love left there at the end. You weren't able to overcome the obstacles. You felt powerless to stop the death of your marriage.

For couples who stay married, things don't appear to be that much better. National studies of married persons reveal a mixed picture. On the one hand, a majority report that they are satisfied and content in their marriages. On the other hand, a majority report that their marriages lack passion and deep intimacy.

Many of you can probably relate to these findings. You are married and have no plans to divorce. You feel happy most of the time. You're not miserable. But you're not as close to your partner as you want to be, either. You want more emotional connection. You want more physical connection. Something's missing from your marriage, isn't it?

Why are millions of marriages ending in divorce? Why are those couples who remain married not as intimate as they want to be? There is an answer, and it may surprise you.

AUTOPSY OF A MARRIAGE

As a Christian psychologist in private practice, I have done autopsies on literally hundreds of marriages. When I see divorced clients in therapy, I take them back for a thorough examination of their failed marriages because they must know what went wrong—what killed the marriage. If they can discover the reasons for the divorce, it's much less likely they will repeat the same mistakes in their current marriage.

In almost every marriage autopsy I've done, I've found the same pattern. Over and over and over again. The couple starts out with infatuation. That brings them together and gets them married. During courtship and the first few years of marriage, they have plenty of physical intimacy and a certain amount of emotional intimacy. They run on the gas of this initial massive burst of hormones and chemistry for four to ten years. Then, the trouble begins. They seem to run out of gas.

Their relationship, which was once so easy, is now much more difficult. They notice, and are increasingly annoyed by, their differences. They can't communicate. They can't solve problems. Without realizing it, they start to play the control-closeness game as described in Chapter Two. She tries to get him to talk, with no success. He tries to get her to have sex, with no success. They slowly pull apart and live separate lives.

They lose their physical and emotional intimacy. It's gone. One of the partners hits the wall first and announces: "I don't love you anymore." After a few halfhearted attempts to patch things up, it's over. They get divorced.

I've shared with you in the previous chapters of this book many techniques to rekindle both physical and emotional intimacy. These techniques do work. But alone, they are not enough to save you from the type of dead marriage I've just described.

I haven't told you the one final ingredient you must have to create the marriage God wants for you. This is the final, essential piece of the puzzle. It will make all my principles (I believe they are *God's* principles, really) come together and work.

SPIRITUAL INTIMACY

I'm talking about spiritual intimacy. It is the lack of spiritual connection which is killing marriages and keeping couples from finding real, genuine intimacy.

In Genesis 2:24 (NAS), God gives us His definition of heterosexual intimacy:

For this reason a man shall leave his father and his mother, and be joined to his wife; and they shall become one flesh.

One flesh is God's idea of intimacy in marriage. What is one flesh? It is a complete coming together of a man and a woman in three areas:

Physically	Two bodies
Emotionally	Two minds
Spiritually	Two souls

God says you have true, complete intimacy only when you are bonded together in all three areas.

The spiritual is the most important part of us as individuals. We are spiritual beings above all else. The spiritual, therefore, must also be the most important part of our marriage relationships.

A large part of my love for Sandy comes from God and the connection we share in Him. On our own, in human strength alone, we simply cannot love each other deeply or consistently. (Neither can you.) Sandy and I tried for years to love each other by human effort. We were Christians then, too! We both loved Jesus Christ. We used relationship techniques to improve our physical and emotional intimacy. They worked to a degree, but not completely. We were running out of gas.

Then we found the answer. Spiritual intimacy. Coming together spiritually has made all the difference for us. We still have problems, of course. We still have to work at our marriage every day. But now we have the power to apply helpful, practical marriage principles. We have the power to love each other. This power does not come from within. It comes from God.

The secret to genuine, lasting intimacy in marriage is becoming one flesh spiritually. I call this spiritual bonding. Spiritual bonding is consistently placing God at the very center of your relationship and growing ever closer to Him as a couple. It is, quite literally, allowing God to work unhindered in your marriage.

When you spiritually bond, God creates genuine intimacy. The best kind, the deepest kind. Even strictly by itself, coming together spiritually as a couple produces a passion and an energy unmatched in human experience. Spiritual bonding also feeds both physical and emotional intimacy. While spiritual intimacy is the most important one-flesh area, the physical and emotional are certainly important, too.

Here's a little-known fact. The main, continuing source of both physical and emotional passion is spiritual bonding. Without the spiritual, you run out of gas in these areas. With the spiritual, you keep on going!

Let me ask you something. Would God make us spiritual beings and then allow us to ignore the spiritual part of the marriage relationship and still have complete satisfaction and intimacy? No. No, He wouldn't. Then doesn't it make sense that if you put God at the center of your relationship, He will bless every other area? That's exactly what He'll do. He's doing it for Sandy and me. He'll do it for you.

How to Spiritually Bond

Here's what you have to do to spiritually bond. There are two prerequisites and four actions.

The first prerequisite is that each person in the relationship must be a Christian. There's a lot of confusion these days about what makes you a Christian. A lot of persons think they're Christians, and they're not.

You are a Christian if you have a personal relationship with the God of the Bible through His Son, Jesus Christ. If you believe Jesus Christ died for your sins (all the things you've ever done wrong) and literally rose from the dead. And if you trust Jesus Christ for forgiveness of your sins.

If you believe these truths, you are a Christian. You know God. You have "passed from death to life." You have the power to live life effectively here on earth. You will live with God forever in heaven after you die.

To spiritually bond, both partners must be spiritually alive. If one partner is spiritually dead, there can be no spiritual bonding. If you are single, do not date and do not marry someone who is not a Christian. You have no idea the grief, the agony, and the disappointment you'll experience if you make this mistake. You can't have spiritual intimacy with a non-Christian partner.

If you are married to someone who is not a Christian, you've got a tough road. You'll have to rely on God's power to get you through. God wants you to stay in the relationship and model Christ (1 Peter 3:1). Keep praying, and have others pray, that your spouse will trust Christ.

The second prerequisite is that each person must be growing spiritually. To know Christ is important. To grow in Him is equally important. You each need to spend individual time with God daily. Establish one specific time each day (morning, lunch hour, evening) where you meet alone with God. Use this time to pray, read the Bible, and maybe use a devotional.

The two of you will grow at different rates. That's okay, as long as you're both growing. A big part of the spiritual bond is sharing the personal growth you each experience. You can't share what you don't have.

The first action in spiritual bonding is that you are honest with each other. Each partner shares in detail, on a regular basis, their own spiritual life, spiritual growth, and spiritual process. Share what you're doing in your daily quiet time with God. Insights gained in your Bible reading. How you're applying the Bible to your life. Your spiritual victories and spiritual defeats. How God is directing and guiding you day by day.

The second action is that you are accountable to each other. Accountability means you voluntarily agree to answer to your partner for your spiritual life. You agree to answer all questions from your partner about your spiritual life. You have no spiritual secrets. You don't open up like this with just anyone. Just with your lifelong partner. And you commit to change and grow spiritually in the ways you and your partner decide are best for you. You set specific spiritual goals, and you report your progress.

Let's say, for example, that I tell Sandy I'll talk to a certain neighbor about Jesus Christ this next week. She'll say: "Great. Let's pray about that right now, and this Saturday I'll ask you how it went."

What are the chances I'll follow through and talk to the neighbor? Very high. Because I made myself accountable. You need to begin meeting together, just the two of you, and being honest and accountable, spiritually.

Men, it's your job as the leader to initiate these meetings. Go to the woman and schedule the meeting. Put it down on your pad and in your planner. Then, at the appointed time, go to her and start the meeting. Start small and build slowly. You could begin with a brief prayer time two or three times a week. Then, you could increase this to four or five times a week. Many couples I know choose to include a time of prayer as part of their thirty-minute talk time each evening.

Picture yourselves on the couch, holding hands and praying. It's a nice picture, isn't it? Then, you could begin to add to the prayer time. You could meet together once a week for fifteen to twenty minutes to read the Bible, read a devotion, pray, and evaluate your spiritual lives for that week.

As you become more comfortable talking spiritually, you'll begin sharing more and more openly your spiritual experiences. You'll weave spiritual bonding into your daily lives. More of your conversations will include the spiritual.

The third action is you worship together. It is a powerful part of the spiritual bond to come together to:

Praise God

Adore God

Pray to God

Meditate on God

Sing to God

I'm talking about public worship. You need to attend church together and worship God in the company of others. It's also important to attend Sunday school together. Interact with others and build relationships.

I'm talking about private worship, too. Just the two of you. In a very private place in your home. Picture this. You put on some praise music and sit on the couch together. You praise God, adore Him for His attributes, pray, and read a passage from the Bible.

You wouldn't do this kind of worship all the time. But maybe once every few months. Try it. See how it goes. I think you'll like it. I know God will.

The fourth, and final, action is you serve God together. This, in my opinion, completes the cycle. Doing things for God as a team brings you closer spiritually in a unique way. This is in addition to whatever you are doing individually for God.

You don't necessarily serve God together all year long. Just part of the year. The best place to serve God together is the local church. It doesn't matter what you do, as long as you do something together that you both enjoy:

> Church nursery
>
> Teaching Sunday school
>
> Evangelism
>
> Discipleship
>
> Visitation
>
> Short-term mission trip

There are also many excellent parachurch ministries: Campus Crusade for Christ, Navigators, Youth for Christ, prison ministry, crisis pregnancy centers, etcetera.

Spiritual bonding is a process. It doesn't happen overnight. It takes time and effort. Everything of value does.

Very few couples spiritually bond, and so very few couples have the one-flesh relationship God talks about in Genesis 2:24. I want you to be one flesh. God wants you to be one flesh. You will never exhaust the intimacy in the spiritual area. Never!

Let me ask two final questions.

Do you have a personal relationship with God through His Son, Jesus Christ? If not, I urge you to establish that relationship now. You can't spiritually bond without it. You can't apply the relationship principles in this book without the power of God in your life.

Are you spiritually bonding with your partner? If not, you will never know true intimacy. I guarantee you that. If you will spiritually bond, you will have the opportunity to experience true, deep intimacy. The best we can have here on earth. I guarantee you that. God guarantees you that.

The choice is yours.

To schedule a seminar or
order Dr. Clarke's audiotapes and videotapes,
please contact:

DAVID CLARKE SEMINARS

www.davidclarkeseminars.com

1-888-516-8844

or

Marriage and Family Enrichment Center

6505 North Himes Avenue

Tampa, Florida 33614

OTHER RESOURCES BY DR. DAVID CLARKE

MARRIAGE
(Video and Audiotape)

MEN ARE CLAMS, WOMEN ARE CROWBARS
Why do men clam up and refuse to talk? Why do women lose interest in sex? What causes the death of romance? Learn what it takes for a couple to connect physically, emotionally, and spiritually.

(Audiotape)

BUILDING A LOVE THAT LASTS
Dr. Clarke teaches how to open up and express emotions, what God says "just to husbands" and "just to wives," and what sexual passion can do for your marriage.

TIGHTENING THE KNOT
Communication, respect, fair fighting, and spiritual unity are interpersonal skills vital to building a passionate, lasting love.

CINDERELLA MEETS THE CAVEMAN
Throw out that old, tired relationship and build a new one that works! Find out how to interact in new, spontaneous ways. Meet your partner's real needs. Learn to face and resolve conflict in a healthy way.

PARENTING
(Video and Audiotape)

WINNING THE PARENTING WAR
Dr. Clarke presents practical, how-to principles that help parents maintain their sanity and raise healthy kids. Topics include: building self-esteem, discipline, and the truth about teenagers.

EMOTIONAL HEALTH
(Audiotape)

LOOKING IN THE MIRROR
The road to intimacy begins with personal change: recovering from losses, "cleaning out" longstanding family issues, developing psychological and spiritual health, and fixing destructive relationship patterns.

Each series, video and audio, contains four talks. To order, call or write:

DAVID CLARKE SEMINARS
6505 N. Himes Avenue
Tampa, Florida 33614
(813) 879-4927